# The Semiautomatic Pistol in Police Service and Self-Defense

by Massad F. Ayoob

D1447317

Available from Police Bookshelf
P.O. Box 122
Concord, N.H. 03302-0122 USA
$9.95 per copy

Second Printing

ISBN 0-936279-07-9

# DEDICATION

*The author owes much of his knowledge and experience to a large number of veteran police officers and weapons trainers, literally too many to list. Three men, however, were especially influential during the formative years of his career. They are:*

*Charlie Smith, former head of nationwide firearms training for the Federal Bureau of Investigation and, after his retirement, founder and first director of the Smith & Wesson Academy;*

*Lt. Frank McGee, for many years commander of the New York City Police Department's Firearms and Tactics Unit; and*

*Deputy Chief Inspector (ret.) of the United States Border Patrol Bill Jordan.*

*The author can never thank these fine and dedicated master lawmen enough for the personal time and insight they gave him and for the uncounted number of officers whom these larger-than-life men saved from violent death. It is to them that this textbook is affectionately and gratefully dedicated.*

# TABLE OF CONTENTS

# FOREWORD

by John H. Pride*

I can remember when I joined the Los Angeles Police Department in 1970, some 18 years ago, but it seems like yesterday when I was issued my brand new Smith & Wesson, 4″, .38 special revolver (double action only, because at the time and still presently, the guns are modified to prevent officers from cocking them in the hope of preventing accidental discharges), and how excited I was to fire it for the first time during training.

I was fresh out of the Army, a Vietnam veteran, breaking into the civilian world again, but not totally, now as a policeman. About four years later I began competing in PPC and met many a shooter and cops from all walks of life. I saw every configuration guns could be modified into, and tried just about every gimmick imaginable. (I got the nickname Mr. Gimmick). As time went on I expanded my competition from PPC to bullseye shooting IPSIC and any type of match I could enter, just for the fun of it.

The main reason I began competing is because of a street shooting I was involved in where I exchanged gunfire with a shotgun-toting suspect, firing my gun five times at the suspect at 40 feet or so and only hitting him once in the shoulder. I wondered why I didn't shoot as well as I did in practice. I decided I needed more practice and to find a way to simulate the stress of a shootout, and competition did just that!

It was in competition where I first had the pleasure of meeting Massad; it was at the Bianchi Cup, 1982 I believe. There was a crowd of shooters, some of them policemen, huddled around this man listening to every word he said. It was Massad giving some tactics tips, or some stress-shooting techniques. Whatever he was talking about, the group was listening!

I had heard of Massad and his traveling school of police tactics, basic self-defense, and advanced auto pistol seminars as well as many other facets of instruction. His background in police work and as a teacher

---

* John Pride is instructor in the semiautomatic pistol for the Los Angeles Police Department. He is former National Municipal Police Revolver Champion and 1987 winner of the Bianchi Cup, the National Action Pistol Shooting Championship.

and writer has impressed me for many years now and his teachings to many of the citizens and police officers throughout the United States have benefited many.

Throughout my years as a firearms instructor and professional pistol shooter, I've met many experts who knew everything about nothing, and spent most of their time ridiculing others in their field rather than listening and experimenting in new areas of shooting and teaching techniques.

In a time when the controversy over which firearm is best for police work is being debated (including yours truly; I debated with Massad in 1986 in American Handgunner over the revolver vs. the auto; I was pro revolver!), Massad has been busy teaching officers how to use the semiautomatic, and now he has put this work into a book.

I've always believed that with the proper training, a semiautomatic pistol in the hands of a police officer or citizen protecting himself or his family has the definite tactical advantage in a STRESS FIRE situation.

Throughout the history of the Los Angeles Police Department, its officers have carried revolvers as their primary sidearm. And, to be honest with you, until 1986, my thoughts on the chances of LAPD switching over to autos were as good as flying your TV to the moon without booster rockets!

In 1986 an LAPD officer, Detective Williams, was picking his son up from school when a suspect that Williams was testifying about in court drove by and shot Detective Williams with a Mac-10 9mm. fully automatic submachine gun, killing him.

It outraged the police community that a police officer, merely doing his job, would get gunned down just to keep him from testifying in court!

This was one of the last straws. Chief Daryl Gates ordered a study into the feasibility of allowing LAPD officers to carry semiautomatic pistols as primary and off-duty weapons. This took guts, knowing that it would cause a stir in the liberal wings and drum up a controversy. But, six months later, the study was completed by Sergeant Jack Schmida and his ordnance unit and the final word was, yes, it can be done!

The ordnance officers spent hours and hours on the phone, talking with agencies throughout the United States that had converted from revolvers to auto pistols, and the questions asked were "How effective have the autos been?" and "How about accidents?" The answers in all cases were positive. Most departments were having total success in the transition, attributed to training.

Now, what guns to choose and what kind of ammunition and what type of training? At first, when a survey was taken of all the officers on LAPD who would be interested in carrying an autopistol, as long as they bought their own guns and equipment and attended a three-day school provided by the Department and on duty status, only 900 officers responded yes. But when the program became a reality, stand-by! 3,000 officers lined up to be added to the training lists. At first it was believed that the semiautomatic would be conducive to more accidental discharges; in ten years LAPD has had some 50 or so accidental discharges with revolvers that shoot double action only!

Since the program went into full swing in June of 1986, over 2,300 officers have switched over to semiautomatics. The Smith and Wesson and Beretta 9mm. pistols are authorized to be carried. For on duty in uniform, the Beretta 92F or the Smith & Wesson 59 series could be carried. This affords the officer 16 rounds with the Beretta and 15 rounds with the Smith & Wesson. A round is carried in the chamber and the officers are taught to fire the first shot double action only, so officers don't cock their weapons. This helps prevent accidental discharges. For off duty, officers can carry any of the Beretta or Smith & Wesson 9mm. pistols.

In one year there has been only one accidental discharge, and in 17 shootings involving officers carrying 9mms the officers have had a definite advantage. Not only in reloading capability, but also in skill. That's right—skill. During the three-day semiautomatic school, officers who would otherwise not even be interested in extra shooting training get training in marksmanship, quick draw, barricade shooting, one-handed shooting, speed reloading and many other skill-enhancing techniques to make them better pistoleroes. The school encourages shot placement and tactics and, surprisingly, it is estimated that nearly the whole LAPD will be carrying autos by the end of 1988. By the way, old revolver man himself, I was assigned to write the lesson plan for the school and teach with the 9mm. cadre. Bill Burroughs of Smith and Wesson Academy flew out to Los Angeles and gave the 9mm. cadre a condensed auto pistol school and greatly assisted in developing our program.

The semiautomatic pistol is the police firearm of the 80s and no doubt will be well into the next century and Massad is right on the mark again with an outstanding book, saving all of you who read it from doing all the footwork in putting your own programs together, or just learning how to do it the right way.

Massad is a street-wise cop and a top pistol competitor who knows what he's talking about, so you can take what he says in this book to be gospel. Believe me, because I've shot with the best of them and have been around the ball park a few times in the field of police work.

A lot of competitors and experts will come and go, but Massad's work will continue to assist police officers to be better cops and to STAY ALIVE.

I look forward to one day teaching with Massad in an advanced auto pistol school; I'm sure he can teach me a few tricks I haven't seen yet.

Every police officer who is considering switching from a revolver to an auto pistol should have this book. I've got mine!

# ABOUT THE AUTHOR

Massad Ayoob got his first Colt .45 automatic for Christmas when he was 12, and the same year began (legally) carrying a concealed, loaded handgun in his family's jewelry store. By the time he got out of college he was captain of a first string pistol team. He won his first state championship at 25, and has since set three national records (2 with HK 9mm. autos, one with a Colt .45 automatic) and become the only man to shoot every Second Chance match since 1976 (almost always with an auto) and one of only four to shoot in every Bianchi Cup since its inception (half with auto, half with revolver). Ayoob is a Master in six separate handgun disciplines, the equivalent of as many black belts in the combat sidearm. A police officer with 14 years experience from patrolman to lieutenant, he began carrying an autoloader on duty in 1973.

Ayoob is presently director of Lethal Force Institute, P.O. Box 122, Concord, NH 03302-0122. He and his cadre staff teach nationwide and in Canada, South America, Europe, and South Africa. Ayoob is a frequently sought court-recognized expert in guns and fatal shootings, and is credited with saving some 20 careers, keeping 7 cops and law-abiding armed citizens out of prison, and saving one man from the electric chair when they had been wrongfully accused after using weapons in self-defense.

Called the "master of officer survival tactics" by Police Marksman Association and labelled a "guru" on the subject by such diverse publications as *The Los Angeles Times, Soldier of Fortune,* and *Gallery* magazine, Massad Ayoob has been quoted or referenced in almost every successful police research proposal to adopt the semiautomatic pistol as a service handgun.

# PRIMARY ADVANTAGES OF THE SERVICE AUTOLOADER

If one were to do a word association test with the average patrolman and say, "autoloader", the most common response would probably be "Firepower!" In fact, analysis of actual use of the auto pistol in the police service shows that firepower is only about third down on the list of the weapon's attributes.

High cartridge capacity and firepower is the most touted auto advantage, but author feels that the collective police experience brings firepower down to #3 on list of auto's most important advantages. This tiny Beretta Jetfire .25, popular as a backup and narc gun, contains nine shots.

Firepower is often the stated reason for switch to autos, but author's research indicates it's third down on the list of real-world advantages. This SIG P-226 carries 15 9mm. hollowpoints in the magazine, a 16th in the firing chamber.

First and foremost comes *improved hit potential under stress.* According to the Police Foundation, a subsidiary of the Ford Foundation, studies of police departments nationwide show a hit potential in street gunfights of approximately 25% with double-action revolvers. That is, of every four shots fired, only one struck the target anywhere on his body. Put another way, 75% of shots fired by revolver-armed police miss the perpetrator and go screaming on through the community.

*Greatest advantage of auto in police service has proven to be superior hit potential under real world gunfighting stress. John Farnam demonstrates in stress exercise with Colt .45 autoloader. Photo courtesy J. Farnam.*

No comparable nationwide study has been done of police departments equipped with autoloaders. The closest we have to such a data base is the closely-monitored Illinois State Police auto pistol experience which began in 1967, and, at any given time from then to now, has involved 1,700 to 2,300 officers armed with Smith & Wesson 9mm. autoloaders. Several generations of ISP leadership generously gave me carte blanche to their files of officer-involved shootings. The fact is that hit potential with the double-action Smith auto was approximately 65%: more than double, nearly triple, the hit potential with the service revolver.

Was this due to excellent training? Not particularly. ISP does in fact have superb firearms training, but no better than LAPD, which averaged 28% hit potential when all patrol officers were armed with revolvers. The difference, ISP and other authorities agree, was the more controllable nature of the semiautomatic pistol in a stress shooting situation. Once the first double-action shot had been fired, the auto pistol cocked itself, and the officer was no longer struggling to keep the weapon steady against a heavy DA trigger pull.

Any police revolver instructor will tell you that the hardest part of his job is training the new officer to hold a two-pound weapon steady as 14 pounds of trigger pressure, moving across nearly an inch of travel, are exerted on the gun. The cocked semiautomatic demands only four to five pounds of pressure, with a much shorter movement. Hence, the gun is not nearly so likely to be jerked off target by the firing stroke as is the DA revolver.

Indeed, many of the 35% misses recorded by ISP in shootouts were with the first shot. Some instructors called the syndrome "fire, miss; fire, hit". For this reason, officers with single-action pistols such as the cocked-and-locked Colt .45 auto have a hit potential even higher than double-action autos, based on the limited data we have.

I say "limited" because no collection base on .45s exists. The only large "police unit" using .45 autos are the military police, and since their weapons are usually carried with the chamber empty and require the slide to be actuated before a shot is fired, their data does not relate to the police sector, where such guns are carried with a round in the chamber. However, in a string of cases the author followed up on recently, .45 auto hit potential in the hands of police has been 100%.

Pima County, AZ: Four shots fired by a sergeant at a murderer who has just mortally wounded a deputy with a .44 Magnum, four solid hits. The suspect is killed instantly.

Los Angeles, CA: Two SWAT team members armed with Colt .45 autos close in on a member of the Aryan Brotherhood who is holding hostages. As he raises his own handgun, the officers fire. One patrolman unleashes three shots, and his partner fires once. The suspect takes four lethal hits and dies instantaneously, before he can harm a hostage. Autopsy shows any of the four shots would have been fatal, three of them at the second of impact.

Patterson, CA: A suspect armed with a Llama .32 auto tries to murder a patrolman, and a sergeant rapidly fires eight shots from his Colt Gold Cup .45. Eight gunshot wounds drop the suspect, fatally.

Littleton, CO: A crazed suspect lunges at an officer with a knife, barely missing him. A brother officer fires one shot from his Colt Combat Commander .45, striking the suspect in the heart and dropping him instantly.

Kamiah, Idaho: A career criminal in the prone handcuffing position turns suddenly and violently on the arresting officer, who fires one shot from his Colt Combat Commander. A single .45 strikes the suspect, inflicting a survivable wound that nonetheless completely terminates all hostilities.

Michigan: An off-duty officer is engaged in a shootout by a gunman carrying a Browning 9mm. auto. The officer draws his WWII-surplus Remington-Rand 1911-A1 .45 auto and fires three shots, striking the suspect three times in the torso and putting him down immediately and fatally.

The list goes on. It does not mean that you can't miss with a cocked and locked .45 auto — one Kentucky narc emptied his 8-shot .45 at a man who had shot his partner, and hit the gunman only twice — but a pattern of solid hit potential emerges, a pattern much more in keeping with professional law enforcement standards than the one-in-four hit potential of the traditional revolver.

*Author discusses police auto advantages with Ed Nowicki, executive director of the American Society of Law Enforcement Trainers (ASLET).*

Is it *just* the gun? There is no centrifuge into which we can throw a gunfight and separate a figure of 20% cartridge effectiveness, 45% superior gun design, and 35% greater skill. In the shooting of the Aryan Brotherhood gunman, the two officers who closed with him were among the finest marksmen on the 7,000 man LAPD, and both had proven their coolness in multiple previous firefights. I have no doubt that if these two SWAT vets had been armed with the Smith & Wesson K-38 uniform revolvers they normally wore during that period, they also could have scored four out of four stopping shots. But both officers feel that the tactical superiority of their .45 autos was a critical reason why they were able to stop him before he killed innocents, and I for one am not arrogant enough to try to gainsay *them*.

Those of us who teach firearms to students who have the option between revolver and auto do see certain patterns, however. The poor shot with a revolver can usually be helped dramatically simply by switching him to a single-action auto. I consider my HK P7 "range gun" to be something of an "orthopedic pistol", particularly for female and small statured male students who have difficulty controlling the double-action revolver. I've lost count of the number of low achievers who, once switched from the six-gun, went to the top five in their twenty-man classes with the P7.

*Shorter trigger reach makes autoloaders, especially the single action variety, ideal performance-builders in the hands of female officers. This policewoman has mastered her Colt .45 sufficiently to compete well against best male shooters at Second Chance National Police Combat Shoot.*

This is confirmed by studies of big police departments that have gone to auto pistols. Virtually without exception, such departments as Illinois State Police have found that *overall shooting competence went up measurably when the officers switched to the automatic, **and the scores of the weakest shooters improved the most dramatically!***

By contrast, Illinois noted that the fine-tuned skills of the department's very best revolver shooters were disrupted by the change in hardware, and that their average scores dropped very slightly. However, virtually all the master shooters were back at their original high averages after they'd had time to acclimate themselves to the new design.

The simple fact is that the auto pistol can be fired with greater speed and accuracy than the service revolver, person for person. There are several reasons for this. First, of course, is the more controllable trigger action.

But other factors enter. Auto pistols generally recoil less than revolvers of equal power. This is because the axis of the bore in the auto is lower in the hand. Since cartridge recoil initially follows the bore line, a lower bore axis gives the gun less mechanical leverage with which to recoil, and therefore dramatically reduces muzzle jump.

*Mild recoil of police autoloaders enhances their effectiveness, reduces greatly the rate of dangerous missed shots. This tester is firing Ruger P-85 9mm. 1-handed from StressFire Kenpo Punch position. Note that while spent casing is just above hammer, muzzle is already back on target for next controlled, rapid fire shot.*

*Fit of pistol or revolver to hand is critical for good performance. Trigger in double action mode is too far forward on this HK P9S for any but the longest fingers to control with acceptable accuracy under stress.*

The auto pistol's grip design and grip-to-barrel angle also fits the average human hand better. The majority of America's best auto pistol shooters fire with the same grips that the factory furnished when they acquired the gun. The vast majority of the best revolver shooters will at least opt for the factory's own oversized grips, and more probably will put on wooden or neoprene replacement grips that better fit their hands. This tells us that auto pistols "feel" better and have less twist in the hand in rapid combat fire than factory-produced service revolvers.

Let us consider the rapid fire competitions such as WSSA (World Speed Shooting Association, or the Steel Challenge-type events) and IPSC (International Practical Shooting Confederation's simulated gunfighting, and the similar Paladin tournament system). In both, the auto pistol reigns supreme, usually the Colt Government type. When time constraints are removed and "whoever hits the target fastest wins", the winner is almost always shooting an auto. On the street, there's no referee blowing whistles to give each of you X amount of time in which to shoot each other, as in police revolver or NRA Action Shooting contests: as in IPSC and WSSA, the fastest center hits win. *Every* major Steel Challenge event and *every* major IPSC event in the history of both sports has been won with single-action auto pistols.

*Combination of better trigger control and higher rate of fire results in revolvers being dumped in favor of autoloaders in any scenario where speed of hits is prized. Here Mike Dalton, foreground, and Steve Nastoff gun down multiple steel targets at Colt Speed Event; both have chosen customized Colt .45 autos.*

The Second Chance National Street Combat Championships for Police was inaugurated in Central Lake, Michigan in 1975. The shooter faces reaction targets (bowling pins), with the gun already in his hand, and starts shooting on signal. Whoever blows the pins off the table fastest wins. The event has been won twice with Smith & Wesson .44 Magnum revolvers, and every other time with Colt or Colt-pattern .45 automatics. Ad Clark, who won the '77 Championship with a revolver, has been carrying a Colt .45 auto on his full-time patrol duties since 1984, by choice. Again, this is telling us something.

Given time, a six gunner with a good sense of rhythm *who knows the time parameters he has to work within* can prevail in a match like NRA Action Shooting, typified by the Bianchi Cup. This is because he can practice semi-rapid, double-action shooting to the point where he can take advantage of the "surprise break, roller trigger" factor of the revolver and shoot more precisely. Again, however, five-second time strings don't occur on the street. It is significant to note that the Bianchi Cup, the one format in which revolvers beat autos, is wrapped up on the last day with the Colt Speed Event. In this big-money match, the top twenty shooters in the Bianchi Cup face off to see who can shoot down man-size steel targets the fastest. While about 15 of the top 20 will have used revolvers in the Cup itself, some 18 of those same 20 in a typical year will bring an automatic to the range the next morning for the Speed Event, and every Speed Event has in fact been won with an autoloader.

## Proprietary Nature to the User

One of every five policemen murdered in the line of duty is killed with his own or his partner's handgun in any given year. In California some years, it has been one out of two, and California generally leads the nation in the number of officers murdered.

A study by the respected police defensive tactics instructors Jordan Roth and Robert Downey of the California Specialized Training Institute in San Luis Obispo studied 138 police officers slain in a ten-year period in America with police guns. 137 were killed with double-action revolvers. Only one, a California narc armed with a Browning Hi-Power 9mm., was killed with his own autoloader. There were no surviving witnesses save the killer, who was never captured, and the question remains whether or not the safety catch was "on" when the weapon was taken from the officer.

The autoloading pistol with manual safety lever is not easy to manipulate into firing position if one is not familiar with the given specimen. Departments that have adopted or authorized automatics have recorded numerous cases in which perpetrators got service guns away from cops and tried to shoot them to death with them, but couldn't accomplish their murderous intentions because they didn't know how to release the safety catches on the stolen autos.

Consider some of the following documented cases:

Tallahassee, FL: A suspect gets an officer's cocked and locked Colt Commander .45 away from him, points it at him, and pulls the trigger. With the thumb safety still engaged, the pistol does not fire. The officer wrestles back his gun and rather firmly stabilizes the situation.

Illinois State Police: Two grand theft auto suspects jump a trooper who is searching the scene of an abandoned stolen car. One grabs him from behind and the other, with both hands, attacks the officer's model 39 Smith & Wesson auto, which is cocked with the safety "off." As he feels the pistol being inexorably pried from his hands, the officer desperately thumbs the magazine release button, dropping the magazine a fraction of an inch in the grip and activating the magazine disconnector safety. The suspect gains possession of the weapon and attempts to shoot the officer several times, but the pistol will not fire. The suspect works the slide, ejecting the live round from the chamber, and again attempts to pull the trigger, without success. The frustrated felons beat the officer unconscious and flee. The pistol, cocked and with the magazine still a fraction of an inch out of place, will be recovered later in their abandoned getaway car; they had still not figured out how to operate it.

Pierce County, Washington: A suspect snatches an officer's Colt .45 automatic and attempts to shoot him with it. He is unable to do so, since the thumb safety is "on". The suspect flees, pursued by the officer, who is given a .38 caliber revolver by a passing motorist who is licensed to carry a concealed weapon. The suspect surrenders at the point of the commandeered weapon.

Illinois State Police: A physically small undercover agent is lured into the back of a van by two dope dealers, who then jump him and disarm him. As his backup officer runs to assist, the suspect who has snatched the Smith & Wesson model 439 pistol tries multiple times to shoot both officers, but is unable to do so: as the gun was being wrenched from his hand, the narc had pressed the magazine release button and activated the disconnector safety. The cover officer strikes the armed assailant over the head with his own service handgun, rendering the perpetrator unconscious, and the second doper surrenders without further resistance.

Salt Lake City, Utah: In the Canyon District, a motorist turns on an officer during a traffic stop and sucker-punches him. Eyewitness testimony is as follows: the attacker reaches down and draws the Smith & Wesson model 39 9mm. automatic from the supine officer's holster, stands over him, points the gun at the officer, and pulls the trigger.

The gun does not fire. The suspect, having apparently seen on TV that you pull back the slide to work an auto pistol, does so: he ejects the live round from the chamber and racks another into its place. Again he pulls the trigger, and again the gun does not fire.

He looks down at the pistol, fumbling with the controls, obviously being aware that auto pistols have safety catches. He paws at the largest lever on the side of the pistol, the slide release. Since the slide is already in the forward position, this accomplishes nothing. Again he aims at the prostrate officer and pulls the trigger, and again nothing happens.

He studiously examines and manipulates the pistol again, finding a button behind the trigger. He presses this button, which turns out to be the magazine release. A magazine with six or seven live 9mm. Luger cartridges now falls out of the pistol, bounces off the would-be cop-killer's foot, and skids under the car, where evidence technicians will recover it later.

Again the gunman points the officer's pistol at him and pulls the trigger. Again, the gun is silent.

The gun-grabber turns his attention once more to the bewildering controls on the side of the gun. Finally, he manipulates the inconspicuous little flat latch on the slide, flipping the thumb safety from "safe" to "fire" position. Exultantly, he aims the weapon at the officer and pulls the trigger.

Nothing happens. Though there is a live cartridge in the firing chamber and the manual safety is "off", the dropped magazine has activated the disconnector safety and the weapon cannot be fired.

The suspect is heard to exclaim "Shit!" and throws the useless pistol at the dazed but alive police officer before he races off. The Canyon District Incident will turn out to be the classic example of a suspect attempting to murder a police officer with his own semiautomatic pistol.

Illinois State Police: A trooper who has stopped two huge, drunk brothers for Driving Under the Influence is attacked by the suspects and dragged off the road into a culvert, where he is savagely beaten and disarmed. One of the brothers snatches his Smith & Wesson model 39 automatic and tries repeatedly to shoot him, not realizing that the safety catch is in the "on" position. He jacks the slide, ejecting a live cartridge and re-chambering a fresh one, to no avail.

A sergeant, notified that one of his troopers is off the air and not responding to dispatch, races to the scene. He finds the two hulking attackers looming over the semi-conscious officer. He orders them to halt, and the one with the gun points it at him, pulling the trigger. His gun does not go off, but the sergeant's model 39 does, and the attacker sprawls backward.

As the officer slides down the hillside into the culvert, the suspect with the pistol gets up again and lunges at the downed officer, placing the muzzle of the stolen gun against him. The sergeant fires a second shot, striking the suspect in the side. He falls unconscious, and later succumbs to his wound. The brother surrenders immediately. Both officers survive the double murder attempt.

New Jersey State Police: A suspect catches a trooper off guard and lunges for his holster, snatching his Heckler and Koch P7M8 9mm. pistol. Spinning adroitly away from the policeman, he points the gun at him and pulls the trigger. There is no shot: the suspect, untrained in the P7's "manual of arms", has failed to depress the cocking lever. The officer jumps his antagonist and, placing his hand over the armed suspect's, manages to turn the pistol toward the attacker's own body. The trooper then closes his hand firmly over the suspect's, activating the cocking lever, and pulls the suspect's trigger finger. The pistol discharges, sending a 9mm. hollowpoint bullet into the attacker's leg. Howling in agony, the suspect falls to the ground, releases the officer's weapon, and surrenders.

Many other instances are on record. In less than fifteen years after the issuance of the Smith & Wesson 9mm. automatic, Illinois State Police had recorded at least nine officers who were alive because the police gun a perpetrator grabbed was a Smith & Wesson auto with safety devices the suspect was unfamiliar with. There is no question in the minds of Illinois State Police command staff that all those officers would have been shot had the snatched gun been a conventional police service revolver. No Illinois trooper has been shot with his own gun by a suspect since the 9mm. auto was adopted.

A study was done in the early 1980s by a Florida police department and published in POLICE CHIEF magazine, the journal of the International Association of Chiefs of Police. Several non-sworn department personnel — secretaries, motor pool, janitorial and clerical personnel — were selected. They ranged from people who had never fired guns to those who owned several of their own.

Each person in the test sample was taken to the department firing range, where they stood at a table on which two loaded guns lay. A few feet away was a silhouette target.

*Police armorer Rick Devoid demonstrates popular cop-killing trick taught in prisons: attacker snatches officer's holstered revolver like this, rips it out of holster, fires upside down. Virtually impossible to accomplish with an auto that has a safety catch, this technique will probably cause **any** auto to jam when slide hits wrist, bottom of hand after first shot has been fired. Another safety advantage of the auto.*

"That target," they were told, "is a police officer. You have just taken his gun. When you hear the signal, raise that gun and shoot the 'officer.' You will try this at least once with each gun."

One of the two guns was a Smith & Wesson model 10 revolver, caliber .38 Special; the other was a Colt .45 automatic, fully loaded, cocked and locked with a live round in the firing chamber.

On the average, the testers were able to pick up the revolver and "kill the officer" in 1.2 seconds. Their average time with the safety-locked automatic was approximately 17 seconds.

It is respectfully submitted that 1.2 seconds is not a lot of time for an officer to react to a violent assault, counterattack, and regain control of his snatched service revolver.

It is likewise suggested that in seventeen seconds, one can do many unpleasant things to the criminal who has snatched one's pistol. . . or, if nothing else, one can run a considerable distance.

To take maximum advantage of this aspect of the auto pistol's "officer survival superiority," the pistol selected should be one with a manual safety catch, and ideally also with a magazine disconnector safety. For obvious reasons, department policy should strongly encourage that the auto pistol be carried with the safety "on".

This last point is widely argued. Smith & Wesson Academy, the training school run by the firm that produces the most popular brand of police auto pistol in use today, suggests that the gun be carried with the safety "off", so that the officer can fire more rapidly and positively in a stress reaction situation. To do so, however, is to sacrifice one of the proven advantages of auto pistol design in the police service. This writer has trained and supervised police officers whom he advised to carry the S&W service automatic with the safety "off", simply because they were too unfamiliar with the gun or too maladroit to rapidly work the safety. One must remember that if one out of five cop-killers use the officer's own gun, that means by definition that the other four out of five bring their own firepower to the gunfight, and the officer *must* be able to quickly and smoothly react with his own weapon.

As this book will emphasize throughout, training must accompany any new piece of equipment. An officer certified years ago on the Breathalyzer was never expected to do breath alcohol tests on a drunk driving suspect with an Intoxilyzer 3000 until he had been retrained with the new equipment. An officer certified to use the simple KR-12 Kustom moving radar gun wasn't turned loose with the more complex VASCAR-Plus speed monitoring device until he'd completed forty hours' training. It follows that an officer who has worked for ten years with a double-action revolver should not be handed an autoloading pistol with one or more safety devices and be expected to go about his duties without similar retraining with the more complex new technology.

However, the properly trained and motivated officer will have no problem flipping the safety catch to the "fire" position on his own weapon when he needs it in a reactive situation. As famed gunfighting authority Jeff Cooper has noted, virtually all contests requiring speed *and* accuracy of first shot have been won with Colt .45 or similar police service automatics, with the shooter wiping the safety into the "fire" position when the draw was complete and the gun was coming up on the target.

This writer has been able to confirm no actual case instance of an officer ever being shot because he could not activate the safety on his service automatic. Many who are leery of the auto pistol concept cite a popular officer survival manual which shows a picture of a young, blond officer slumped against a pile of cans in a supermarket, a "safety-on" Smith & Wesson 9mm. automatic lying beside him, and clutching a bloody "death wound" at his throat. The caption of that photo reads, "This officer died because he was unfamiliar with a semiautomatic. When he tried to defend himself during a robbery, he forgot the safety was engaged."

That would be enough to make you scuttle auto pistols forever. . . if you didn't know the truth behind the picture. The man in the photo is a model. The still is from a scene in a firearms handling safety film that was produced by the author of the survival manual some years before the book came out. *No such incident ever actually occurred.*

As near as this writer can determine, the inspiration for the actor to do that part in the firearms handling film came from an incident that occurred in Northern Heights, Illinois. A CHPD officer, newly issued a Smith & Wesson 9mm. autoloader and not fully trained with it, tried to shoot a fleeing car thief. Neglecting to release the safety, he was unable to get a shot off. The officer was not injured nor was he in danger. Indeed, his failure to be familiar with his equipment probably saved him and his police department from a monstrous lawsuit.

This writer does not wish to impugn the motives of the authors of that book and that film; they wanted to warn officers what *could* happen. The point is, that it *didn't* happen. We concur with the authors that semiautomatic pistols should not be issued to officers so undertrained or so incompetent that they would forget to thumb the safety catch before they fired. However, I would submit that any professional police officer issued an automatic would quickly learn to release the safety before he pulled the trigger, as surely as he has learned to put his cruiser in gear before he steps on the accelerator. Either way, "the equipment won't go" if you don't "prep" it first.

The safety catch feature is at once a great strength and a great weakness in the auto pistol. The strength is that a punk who grabs your gun probably won't know how to make it fire before you can take it back. The weakness is that if you're a stupid punk yourself, and trying to protect the public and yourself with equipment you're unfamiliar with, it may not work for you either. The argument that "you have to release a safety before you fire" is one that is invariably heard when officers ask if they can be allowed to carry auto pistols.

I personally believe that someone too stupid to release the safety on his pistol before he pulls the trigger, and so uninterested in safety that he won't learn how his own gun operates, is not a good candidate for a job that requires him to operate high-powered automobiles and sophisticated radar equipment, and to make split-second decisions upon which human lives and reputations will depend.

In any case, that is a moot point. If the argument over the safety catch feature becomes the final insoluble issue when debating whether or not autos will be allowed by a given department, two very satisfactory alternatives exist. One is to adopt a weapon like the SIG-Sauer which has no safety catch and fires with the first pull of the trigger just like a revolver. True, the officer loses the "proprietary nature to the user feature", but he at least has a service handgun that shoots eight to sixteen times instead of five or six times, and which is more controllable in rapid combat fire.

*Department need not restrict officers to a single autoloader. Lt. Ayoob, left, wears cocked and locked Colt .45 auto in LFI Concealment Rig for plainclothes duty, while his chief Cameron Harbison is armed with S&W 669 9mm. in Bianchi hi-ride duty holster. LAPD, Las Vegas Metro, Arizona Highway Patrol, and many other agencies give their officers a choice of approved service automatics.*

*"Let those who ride decide." Service revolvers and service autos integrate well on the police firing line. Open policy allows officers to carry weapons they have the most personal confidence in.*

The other alternative is to issue or approve a gun that has an option of "either/or", such as the Smith & Wesson in 9mm. or .45. The officer who worries about being able to get his safety off can simply leave it in the "fire" position with a late generation gun like the S&W 645, 639, 659, 439, 459, 469, 669, etc. The officer armed with any of those same guns who worries about being disarmed may have the option of carrying *his* issue gun with the safety catch in the "safe" position. The history of law enforcement is that while the rules are paramilitary, the job is done by individuals. This should be reflected in policy by letting the individual officer carry the weapon he or she is most confident and competent with, in the *manner* with which they are most confident and most competent.

## Firepower

In real-world usage of the police service automatic pistol, firepower has clearly been shown to be third down on the list of the gun's advantages. Yet there is no question that many departments would not have adopted it and had cops saved by its superior hit potential or its proprietary nature to the user had they not been initially swayed by the firepower argument.

At least three major law enforcement agencies switched to the auto pistol solely on the basis of firepower. The best known is the New Jersey State Police. NJSP trooper Philip Lamonico, considered a "supercop" by his brethren, was killed in a firefight with two radical leftists who supported themselves and their self-serving "cause" by armed robbery. Both perpetrators were armed with 15-shot 9mm. automatics. Lamonico emptied his 6" Ruger .357, loaded with .38 Special hotloads, without striking his opponents; they shot him nine times on his bulletproof vest and slipped one more slug between the seams and into his heart, killing him.

NJSP troopers were outraged. They demanded shotguns in the patrol cars (granted almost instantly by high command) and pushed strongly for high-capacity 9mm. automatics. Union head Tom Iskzyricki's demands were heard by Colonel Clinton Pagano, head of the department. An exhaustive study of police handguns was done at the NJSP Academy at Sea Girt, New Jersey, and when it was over, each trooper was carrying a Heckler and Koch P7M8, an 8-shot 9mm. Parabellum autoloader with a ninth round in the chamber. . . and each trooper had four spare 8-round mags to back him up for a total of 49 rounds of fast firefight potential. The feedback this writer has received from the troopers has been overwhelmingly positive.

Interestingly, since the Lamonico tragedy Jersey troopers have not gotten into another high-volume firefight requiring more than six pistol shots. However, the easy-hit potential of the P7M8 allowed one trooper to stop a gunfight with a single bullet that pierced his adversary's heart and killed him instantly, and saved another from certain death when his gun was taken away and turned on him by a man who didn't understand the P7M8's design well enough to make it go off. The trooper in that case grabbed the gun while still in the attacker's hands, turned it toward his antagonist, and shot him.

This is the history of the auto pistol in the police service: acquired for its firepower, it shows its greatest strength in hit potential and in being "non-user friendly" to cop-killers who snatch the gun from the officer.

NJSP was not the only department to go to the autoloader based on firepower. While the ostensible reason for the trend-setting switch of Illinois State Police to 9mm. automatics was to give them a gun equally suitable for on- and off-duty carry, it is a little known fact that an incident some years before may have had at least as much to do with it.

In the '60s, an officer of the ISP got into a running gunfight with a suspect who was armed with a Colt .45 automatic. The trooper, who had ducked behind a tree to reload his six-shot revolver, looked up in horror to see that the suspect had run to his police cruiser and was about to drive off with it. To lose your cruiser ranks with losing your gun when you're a cop: the ultimate humiliation that you'll just about die to prevent.

This one did die to prevent it. His open revolver still unloaded in his hand, he abandoned the cover of his tree and ran to the patrol car. Seeing that the trooper's revolver was disabled and he was helpless, the undoubtedly amused criminal waited until the trooper rounded the front of the patrol car and then shot him through the heart with the .45. The mortally wounded trooper was in fact able to run back around the front of the car, down the full length of its right side, and reach the trunk where he was trying to get at his stowed shotgun, before he ran out of oxygenated blood and died. The cop-killer was slain by other state troopers the following day, but the lesson was unquestionably in the mind of then-Sgt. in charge of Ordnance Louis Seman when he wrote the history-making proposal to equip the Illinois State Police with fast-shooting, fast-reloading 8-shot 9mm. automatics.

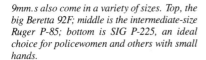

*9mm.s also come in a variety of sizes. Top, the big Beretta 92F; middle is the intermediate-size Ruger P-85; bottom is SIG P-225, an ideal choice for policewomen and others with small hands.*

It has never been officially confirmed, but there is an interesting story told by LAPD officers about why they were finally allowed to carry 9mm. automatics on patrol. For decades, the LAPPL (Los Angeles Police Protective League, the patrolmen's union) had fought fiercely for the right to carry automatic pistols or, at least, more potent cartridges in their .38 service revolvers. They were thwarted at almost every turn, twice being thrown as bones new .38 loads that were only slightly more street-effective than the round-nose lead bullets that so many officers had had to fire six or more of into felons to make them go down.

That changed after a shooting in the mid-1980s in LA's Chinatown. Two patrolmen walked into a cramped jewelry store that was being held up by multiple perpetrators, and the tiny shop exploded into gunfire.

One officer emptied his revolver, reloaded, emptied it again, and had reloaded a second time and was coming up to continue fire when he was shot in the throat and put out of the fight. The other officer had fired several rounds and reloaded when he took a bullet through the side that found his heart and killed him.

Later, when the surviving hero cop was about to receive his medal of valor, he reportedly told Chief Daryl Gates in private, "Chief, if we'd had 14-shot 9mm. automatics, we probably both would have walked out of there." Gates, a boss who had come up through the ranks and was acutely sensitive to the needs of his men, is said to have been deeply moved. Suffice to say that it was at about this time LAPD began in earnest its study of the 9mm. auto pistol in the police service, culminating with the early-1986 announcement that officers so disposed who were willing to take extra training would be allowed to carry high-capacity Beretta or Smith & Wesson 9mm. autoloading pistols. By 1987, it was announced that the chief wanted all 7,000 LA cops, or at least as many as possible, to be carrying 9mm. autos by the end of 1988.

Just because firepower is the least important of the real-world, primary advantages of the auto pistol doesn't mean it is a myth. Those who oppose the auto pistol in the police service will tell you, "Firepower is not a substitute for tactics".

They miss the point. *Firepower is a COMPONENT of tactics,* and this has been so since the first two Cro-Magnon tribes began throwing rocks at each other and realized that whoever threw the most rocks the fastest and the most accurately generally won. More recently, the longbow at the Battle of Agincourt, the Maxim machine gun of WWI that chopped the previous century's vaunted horse cavalry into dog meat, and in WWII, the semiautomatic M-I Garand rifles of American troops that laid waste to both Japanese and German infantry in any sort of equal combat that pitted Garand-equipped Yanks against Axis soldiers armed with obsolete bolt-action rifles. . . the history of armed conflict shows that those who can throw the most missiles the fastest and the most effectively, prevail.

The history of drawn-out police gun battles shows this, too. In the SLA shootout in Los Angeles, the full-automatic M-2 .30 caliber guns of the Symbionese Liberation Army sent a much larger contingent of LA's elite SWAT cops to ground, until caravans could be sent to headquarters to get machine guns for the cops themselves. By the time it was over, more cops with more guns firing faster — over five thousand shots worth, plus pyrotechnic chemical munitions — had finally put the SLA safehouse under.

At the end of the Roaring Twenties and in the beginning of the Dillinger years, lightweight punks like Dillinger, Baby Face Nelson, Pretty Boy Floyd, and Bonnie and Clyde were able to terrorize local police only because they had looted National Guard armories and bigger police departments of fully automatic weapons. Knowing you were pitting a .38 revolver against men armed with Browning Automatic Rifles and Thompson submachine guns, would *you* relish chasing them with the declared intent of either killing them or depriving them of their freedom? It's little wonder that it took squads of Hoover's fledgling FBI agents, just as heavily armed, to bring such criminals to bay.

The desperadoes of the Thirties were a boon to police equipment dealers. Dillinger and his ilk were Thompson's most successful salesmen of fully automatic weapons to law enforcement agencies. The trend died out by the postwar years, and chiefs in the Fifties and Sixties who inherited arsenals of Remington automatic shotguns and Thompson submachine guns were apologetic, as if they were red-faced about a paranoid and senile old grandfather whose name they'd just inherited.

Yet, by the beginning of the Eighties, things had taken another 180° turn. Incidents like the Norco bank robbery in California, the depredations of the SLA, and the combined Weather Underground and Black Liberation Army robbery of a Brink's truck in Nyack, NY had written in dead policemen's blood the fact that today's criminals were ready to pick up heavy weapons, use paramilitary tactics, and slaughter responding patrol officers without compunction.

All of a sudden, it was socially acceptable within law enforcement circles to put a Mini-14 rifle in the patrol car and to reconsider the fact that the lone officer patrolling a remote sector might just have to hold the fort against multiple heavily armed perpetrators until backup could arrive and might just have some reasonable need for a high-firepower weapon after all.

The Seventies and Eighties brought another deadly echo of the Dillinger years: criminals wearing "bulletproof vests". In 1972, Richard Davis invented the soft, always-wearable, concealable body armor he called "Second Chance". He sold it to cops only, but dozens of imitators got into the act and sold their cheap but functional copies to anyone with the money. By the late 1970s, the concealed bulletproof vest was as standard among cocaine dealers as the gold-plated spoon and Federal intelligence in 1980 would indicate that during the Hell's Angels national "run", at least half of the outlaw bikers were wearing concealed, soft armor of the type originally designed for police patrolmen. The infamous Brink's Nyack shootout underscored the point: a Nyack sergeant put a .38 slug dead on his attacker's sternum, only to be murdered by terrorist fire; when a bullet to the head killed his assassin at a police roadblock later, the gunman was found to be wearing a Kevlar vest, and the flattened-out police bullet that had stopped on it was in his shirt pocket, kept as a souvenir.

Against heavily armed and armored perpetrators who work in squads, the lone officer equipped only with a six-shot revolver is terribly disadvantaged. The Colt .45 automatic, that fires eight times without reloading and can be reloaded in as little as a second (three seconds' time for an "average-trained" officer) gives him a much bigger chance against overwhelming odds. The pistol that shoots fourteen to seventeen times without reloading has a tactical edge that need not even be discussed.

*Reliable function and "maintenance-friendly" stainless steel construction mark two of the best .45 service automatics: S&W's model 645 double action, left, and Colt's Government series '80 SS cocked and locked at right.*

Does firepower make a difference if the single officer faces two or three armed criminals? It doesn't take a pocket calculator to figure it out, but that machine or a computer can help convince the modern chief of police on paper that the auto pistol has a definite firepower advantage.

It is you against three men. You are armed with a six-shot revolver. They are armed with "whatever". Police Foundation studies, backed up by those of NYPD and LAPD, indicate that you will have to fire four times to hit one man once with a revolver. If you're up against only *two* armed men, therefore, *the proven odds are that you'll get only one of them!* This leaves you with an empty gun facing an armed, and rather ticked off, survivor of the armed robbery team. . . and that's when you're facing only two of them.

Let's try that again. Same situation: you're up against two or three armed criminals, but this time you have a semiautomatic pistol. The worst odds, *according to actual police gunfights*, is that about two out of three of your shots will hit the opponent. With a 9-shot HK P7, you'll have fired three times at each of your three assailants and hit them each twice. People shot twice in the vital zone with 9mm. police hollowpoints are not famous for their ability to continue effective fire against respond-ing officers. If it's only two assailants, you've hit them three times apiece. Compare this with a likelihood of having hit with only 1.5 out of six shots.

Even the stoutest revolver fans don't argue whether or not firepower favors the autoloader. They only suggest that firepower is not a factor in the equation.

Be realistic. Consider the fact that armed robberies are increasingly perpetrated by drilled teams instead of lone offenders. Ask yourself if your officers might ever have to deal with a gang of armed outlaw bikers. True, that's a worst case scenario, but your officers carry guns only *for* worst case scenarios.

Let us go back to the problem of the offender that wears a bulletproof vest. There are half a dozen ways or more to deal with him, but relatively few of those approaches are morally or practically acceptable in law enforcement.

If the offender who faces your officer wears a vest, your man has two choices: try to shoot *through* the vest, or try to shoot *around* it.

Let's say shooting through the vest is Plan A, and shooting around it is Plan B.

A-1: *Carry an armor-piercing bullet.* This is an amusing suggestion, given the fact that the only major police department that ever *did* issue armor-piercing bullets, the Utah State Police, abandoned them because they never did face an armored felon but always kept coming up against perpetrators face to face, who just twitched when the armor-piercing bullets skidded through them and kept shooting. The requirements for an armor-piercing bullet — superhard, pointy and non-expanding nose — are diametrically opposed to what is needed in a good *man-stopping* bullet, which is likelihood of staying inside the body, delivery of all possible energy to the target, and reduced potential of ricochet if the bullet misses. While armor-piercing bullets have a place in the police arsenal for SWAT cops facing barricaded felons or as a backup load for lone officers in remote rural areas, they are not the load that should be in the gun at the moment of the encounter.

Detroit police sergeant Evan Marshall has publicly stated that he always carried one last-ditch magazine of armor-piercing 9mm. for worst-case-scenario gunfights. I used to carry KTW armor piercing as the last magazine for my police service .45 automatic. I felt, as Evan must have, that if I had emptied a couple of magazines and my antagonist was still moving around, he must either be behind something solid by now, or wearing a bulletproof vest. Call it arrogance. The department I now work for forbids armor-piercing ammo and I no longer carry it on duty, instead loading my pistol and ammo pouches with department-approved loads.

Suffice to say that carrying armor piercing in the gun — and really, that's what you're going to be firing when it hits the fan — is stupid. Most times, you will be facing a soft-skinned mammal instead of something ensconced behind Kevlar or steel, and armor piercing will just bump your soft-skinned killer and convince him that since you've mortally wounded him, he'd better kill you now even if he wasn't going to before.

A-2: *Use High Powered Rifles.* If I had to go on stakeout for guys I knew to be armored, you'd better *believe* I'd be armed with a high-powered, semiautomatic rifle, the velocity of which negates any concealable vest now made. They're bulletproof against pistols and shotguns, folks, not .308s and .223s.

Alas, you can't walk on patrol with a 7.62mm. (.308 caliber) assault rifle unless your tour of duty is in South America. The police department I serve is half an hour away from the Laconia bike races, which are right up there with Sturgis and Daytona on the outlaws' calendars, and you'd better believe I've got a scoped 7.62mm. in my trunk during that period; but I don't keep it in my hand or on my person unless there's a danger call. We need to address the service *handgun*, the weapon the officer will always have with him or her when danger strikes suddenly: a reactive weapon, not a pro-active one like my rifles.

Carrying armor-piercing ammo in a regular firefight, even if you survive, creates an unacceptable danger to bystanders. Consider the grim joke I tell my students about having to shoot a thin-skinned perpetrator with armor piercing: "This is car 54, I need an ambulance at First and Main. . . an ambulance at Second and Main. . . and, uh, an ambulance at *Third* and Main. . ."

A-3: *Use Exotic Handguns.* I've tested a Dan Wesson police service revolver rechambered for the .256 Winchester Magnum cartridge. It would shoot a bullet through one side of a vest, through the man in between, and might or might not be captured for evidence on the other side of the vest, though that would be a moot point. But, despite some of the best brains in firearms engineering working on the problem, pressure inside the gun was so high that you couldn't extract the casings by hand to reload. It just wasn't a fighting handgun. Fact: there's no specialty cartridge made that will fill the demands of the police service and still stop inside an unarmored man while also going through a bullet-proof vest. The closest we have to this are the 125-grain semijacketed Federal, Remington, and Winchester .357 Magnum hollowpoints, which stop on a top-quality Second Chance Y2+ vest but will rip through the cheap imitations and kill anything behind it, yet will mushroom in pure flesh and stay inside as a general rule when you have to shoot an unarmored suspect. The German GAS round (Geco Action Safety, known in the US as the BAT, or Blitz Action Trauma) in 9mm. Parabellum does in its caliber proportionately what the 125-gr. SJHP does in .357 Magnum.

We go then to Plan B: shooting the armored felon outside his area of protection.

B-1: *The Mozambique drill.* Developed by a well-known U.S. pistol instructor, the Mozambique drill was inspired by an incident in which a troopie in Africa shot a terrorist twice in the chest with his 9mm. service automatic. The "terr" kept coming, and the trooper fired a third shot, striking his opponent in the neck and putting him down. The American instructor's Mozambique drill calls for the officer to "fire two shots in the chest, lower the weapon to analyze what is happening, then come up and carefully place one more shot in the opponent's forehead."

Many officers like the Mozambique as a "Plan B" drill for the PCP freak or armored suspect who has not be deterred by bullets in the torso. LAPD has adopted the technique, as have other agencies.

However, there are numerous shortcomings in the Mozambique. First, the Ohio Attorney General's office ordered the state's Peace Officer Training Academy to stop teaching the technique, on the grounds that it constituted shooting to kill instead of shooting to stop. The final shot to the head was seen as a coup de grace, not a response to stopping failure.

Second, charges of genocidal intent have been raised by black militant groups after the shootings of blacks by white officers. In such a scenario, an officer who had trained with a technique call "Mozambique" is not in the strongest defense posture in court.

Third, the "lowering the gun to assess the situation" between the second and third shots is ridiculous. Does the officer expect a digital readout to appear on the suspect's chest saying, "Beep — .18% blood alcohol content, unknown quantity PCP, Second Chance vest"? The officer who lowers his gun at this critical point will see only a man firing at him. He has *already* assessed the situation: a man he has shot twice in the chest is still firing at him! There is nothing further to analyze. If the officer is going to try for a head shot, he should do so immediately without hesitation.

Fourth, the head is a small, bobbing target, difficult to hit even on stationary silhouette targets. Facing a living human being, it becomes close to impossible. When the officer's weapon points at the suspect's face, the suspect's body alarm reaction will instinctively snap the head down or to the side, out of harm's way, while the officer is "carefully" lining up his shot.

B-2: *Modified Mozambique.* A more realistic approach to the Mozambique technique is to fire twice to the torso and then, if the suspect is still upright and fighting, fire *two shots immediately at the head.*

The original Mozambique requires three hits per suspect. Armed with a double-action six-shot revolver, the officer is unlikely to get the two chest shots and the head hit, based on the Police Foundation's 25% hit potential figure. Armed with a nine-shot autoloader with a 65% hit potential, chances are much greater that the three hits will be achieved.

In the modified Mozambique, four shots per suspect are called for. Stats show us that with the revolver, only one of those bullets can be expected to connect. With the service autoloader's combination of greater firepower and better hit potential, the officer stands a vastly greater chance of putting enough of the four rounds where they need to go.

B-3: *LFI Technique.* Recognizing the difficulties of the Mozambique in any of its forms, Lethal Force Institute has from its beginning taught a different "stopping failure response". This is two shots in the torso, followed immediately by two rounds to the pelvis if the perpetrator remains up and fighting. The advantages are as follows:

The pelvis is a much easier target to hit. An hour on the range will convince any police firearms instructor that the rank and file officer can place two shots in the torso and two more in the pelvic zone faster than he can put two in the chest and miss the third shot to the head.

The pelvis cannot be effectively ducked out of the officer's line of fire, as the felon's head can and will be. The best the perpetrator can do is turn sideways, giving the officer an even more devastating angle of fire that can shatter both hips.

As any orthopedic surgeon will attest, if a man's pelvis is broken, his body support structure is violated, and the man will fall. Obviously, a shattered lower body does not keep a suspect from firing. However, a falling man is like a dog with its feet off the ground: he is disoriented and unable to function effectively. Once he is down, however, he can now fire somewhat effectively from the ground. This was proven when one of my students led a contingent of officers through the door of a drug house and was shot in the hip by a suspect armed with a Smith & Wesson model 10 loaded with 158-grain round-nose .38 bullets. As the cop pitched forward, the suspect turned his attention toward the next officer. It was his last act: firing from the floor, my student emptied his 9mm. Browning Hi-Power into the perpetrator, striking him fourteen times in perhaps three seconds and killing him outright. The officer today walks with only a trace of a limp.

Therefore, an officer using the LFI technique should be prepared to fire a fifth or sixth shot to "anchor" a downed suspect who is still trying to shoot. It will be found that once the suspect is down, the dead weight of the body severely limits the ability to snap the head out of the line of fire. A brain shot now becomes viable.

Obviously, though, this technique requires an even greater expenditure of ammunition than the Mozambique. The auto pistol, with its 65% or better hit potential and larger reservoir of ammo, is almost mandated even for a confrontation with a lone perpetrator who is armored with Kevlar or chemicals, *let alone for multiple foes of this type*. Clearly, then, no matter what emergency response technique is called for, the auto pistol possesses a great tactical advantage over the revolver when the officer faces a suspect who is capable of absorbing large quantities of lead due to body armor, adrenaline high, or intoxication with drugs or alcohol.

In summary, then, the semiautomatic police service pistol offers four primary advantages over revolver technology:

1) Dramatically increased hit potential under stress, with concomitantly great reduction in the number of wild shots fired by police officers;

2) Proprietary nature to the user, making it extremely difficult for a suspect who snatches a police officer's automatic to shoot the officer or anyone else;

3) Increased firepower which, coupled with improved hit potential, vastly increases the officer's survivability in a firefight, particularly with multiple opponents; and

4) Superior tactical ability to neutralize suspects high on drugs, wearing body armor, or capable for other reasons of absorbing many shots before going down.

While these are the most significant advantages of the service auto pistol, the concept has other important strong points as well. They will be addressed in the next chapter.

# SECONDARY SEMIAUTOMATIC PISTOL ADVANTAGES

While hit potential, resistance to gun grabs, firepower, and tactical potential are the most critically important attributes of the service auto, the concept has numerous other advantages in police work as well. These include superior adaptability to plainsclothes wear, superior night-firing characteristics, more relevant practice and training, ease of repair, ease of jam clearing and, in some cases, greater confidence and greater deterrent effect on suspects.

Adaptability to plainclothes wear was the ostensible reason why Illinois State Police in 1967 became the first large police agency to adopt the semiautomatic. At the time, all Illinois troopers were expected to be armed 24 hours a day. Colt and Smith & Wesson revolvers of 4" to 6" barrel length were standard uniform weapons, and the same makes of 2" .38 revolvers were the general choice for off duty. When required to qualify with their plainclothes guns, however, average scores fell to 217 of 500 possible, compared to an average of 393 out of 500 with the duty weapon.

*Autoloaders come in a variety of sizes for duty, plainclothes use. Two popular choices are these stainless Colt .45s, full size Government Model (top) and compact Officer's Model.*

Sgt. Louis Seman, at that time head of Ordnance for the department, felt a service automatic would be flat and compact enough for round-the-clock carry, giving the trooper a single all-purpose weapon the department could qualify him with. The Colt Government Model was deemed too heavy, though the lightweight Colt Commander was a strong candidate. The double-action feature of the S&W model 39 was what decided Seman on that weapon. Average scores with it were 374 out of 500.

*(Left) Flat silhouette and concealment make modern service autoloaders compact enough for double function as plainclothes off-duty weapons. (Right) Author's T-shirt conceals full size Colt Government Model Series '80 .45 auto in LFI Concealment Rig by Ted Blocker.*

Ironically, shortly after the adoption of the model 39, the requirement to be armed at all times was rescinded. Off-duty carry was still permitted, however, and while most officers did carry the 39 on their own time — usually "Mexican style", simply thrust into the waistband — some troopers felt the gun a bit too bulky and in any case wanted a second weapon for backup on the job. In the late 1970s ISP authorized Colt and S&W .38 and .357 revolvers for off-duty and backup carry as alternatives to the 9mm. auto, so long as the officers qualified with them.

Elsewhere, many officers have come to appreciate the flat silhouette of the service auto, which makes it much more comfortable and discreet in concealed carry than revolvers of comparable power. When carried concealed, particularly on the belt, the thick bulge of a full-sized revolver's cylinder and the flared, square edge of its grip make concealment difficult. A 9mm. or .45 auto, even a full-sized military-style pistol, hides much more effectively.

At least one police department, Waltham, Massachusetts, PD, originally bought S&W model 59 autos for only its plainclothesmen while keeping revolvers in the uniform holsters. The feeling mirrored that of ISP nearly a decade before: it was the man in plainclothes who got the biggest advantage from the powerful, easy-to-shoot, yet more concealable autoloader.

Some departments have taken an opposite tack. After Riverside issued model 59 9mm.s to all uniformed officers, plainclothesmen were given the choice of the new autos or their old snubnose .38 revolvers. Two detectives armed with the latter were serving a warrant on a paraplegic who was in a wheelchair due to wounds received in his last shootout with police. Taking the detectives by surprise, the man drew a cheap .38 and shot both, killing one and wounding the other. The wounded investigator emptied his 5-shot Chief Special at the suspect without effect and ran into another room. He had no spare ammo with which to reload. The suspect picked up the dead investigator's .38, crawled after the wounded man, and finished him off. Many officers in Riverside felt that the 9mm. auto — easier to shoot than a small revolver for even a wounded man, and containing three times as many cartridges as the Chief's Special — might have allowed the second officer to win the firefight and recover from his wounds. They have also speculated that the killer, whose own gun was empty when he killed the second cop, might not have been able to operate a safety-locked 9mm. auto had that been the gun he took from the body of the first officer.

*Superior night-firing characteristics* are another auto-pistol advantage. Most police gunfights occur in some degree of darkness, and the brighter the officer's muzzle flash, the less effectively he can place his shots in the dark. Auto pistols uniformly burn their gunpowder more efficiently inside their gun barrels than police revolvers in most calibers, and therefore flash less in the dark. It is powder that is still burning beyond the muzzle that causes muzzle flash.

*Reduced muzzle flash compared to equivalent revolver loads, excellent pointing characteristics, ease of reloading by feel, and more manageable trigger pulls combine to make the auto a superior night shooting weapon. Author shot this 60-round group in a Julio Santiago Police Nightshooting target with his Colt Lightweight Commander .45, customized for police service by gunsmith Bill Laughridge.*

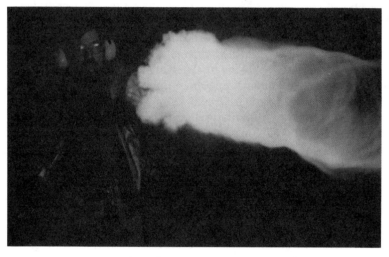

### Volume I of
### *Gunfighting for Police:*
### *Advanced Tactics and Techniques*

### *by Massad F. Ayoob*
### *with foreword by Ray Chapman*

Observe the cover of the book, "StressFire". In that picture, the author is firing a 4″ S&W model 13 with 125-grain Federal .357 Magnum ammunition. The vortex-like fireball is the sole illumination for the photo. A muzzle flash of that magnitude can functionally blind some officers for up to five seconds.

The relative muzzle blasts of .38 Special +P and +P+ ammo should be compared to the "flash signatures" of .45 ACP and 9mm. It will be noted that the autos have much less disturbing muzzle flashes. A .45 ACP is an ideal nightfighting weapon, since with a 5″ barrel it gives barely enough muzzle flash to silhouette the gunsights for an instant, giving the officer feedback on whether or not his aim was true. When one police department (Weare, NH) switched from the S&W m/686 4″ .357 Magnum revolver to the same firm's 5″ m/645 auto in .45 ACP, video comparisons of night shooting characteristics were the final deciding factor.

*Practice and training are more relevant with autoloaders* than with revolvers, because many officers still train with mild wadcutter or standard velocity .38 ammo, but actually carry hot +P or Magnum rounds on duty. As early as the Newhall Massacre of 1970 in which four California Highway Patrolmen were murdered, training with light loads but carrying powerful ones has been identified as a factor in officer deaths in gunfights. No record shows that any of the four patrolmen ever trained with any round more powerful than target .38 wadcutters, yet three of the four were carrying Magnum loads that fatal night. Only Patrolman Frago, the first to die and the only one to be killed without firing a shot, had .38 Special ammo in his gun. Officer Gore fired his .357 Magnum and missed, and was killed seconds later by two .38 Special bullets. Officer Pence fired all six of his .357 Magnum rounds without once touching a suspect, and was killed with a .45 automatic as he reloaded. Officer Allen fired his shotgun until it malfunctioned, then triggered five .357 Magnum rounds before being mortally wounded by buckshot blasts. None of his .357 bullets found their target, and only a single partly spent double-0 pellet struck one perpetrator, inflicting a superficial wound that only served to further enrage him. Subsequent to this incident, among other changes, CHP personnel were permitted to carry only .38 Specials, and training soon focused on qualifying with the hot +P+ ammo that was issued for patrol. It is felt that the unaccustomed bright muzzle flash, powerful recoil, and explosive reports of their .357s contributed to the fact that the embattled Patrolmen in Newhall failed to neutralize their assailants before being killed.

This tragic phenomenon is virtually impossible with the auto pistol. This is because only full-powered ammunition will cycle the slide of a typical service automatic. The gun will jam constantly if the officer or his supervisors attempt to "fudge training with wimp loads". Thus, every round fired in training and practice by the auto-equipped officer is meaningful and job-related in that it replicates the blast and recoil of the load he will be using if he must ever defend his life or the lives of the citizens he serves.

*Ease of repair* is another advantage of the auto pistol. Designed original-ly as a battlefield gun that would daily be field-stripped for cleaning by troops, and would have to be repairable with standard replacement parts by armorers of limited training, the auto can stand to have most of its parts replaced on a "drop-in basis" without precision fitting with hand tools. This is by no means true of the double-action revolver, whose mechanism requires considerable fine fitting by a highly trained and well-equipped armorer.

Suffice to say that the great majority of police officers who are issued revolvers are told, "Never field-strip your service revolver any farther than taking the cylinder out. If it needs to be taken apart, let the depart-ment armorer or contract gunsmith do it!" By contrast, virtually every police officer issued a semiautomatic pistol learns on the first day of orientation how to thoroughly field-strip, clean and lubricate, and reassemble his own sidearm. This also tends to increase the individual officer's confidence in the working of his weapon and his understand-ing of that operation.

While it is true that some autoloading pistols are more likely to "jam" than the average revolver, it is also true that *most auto pistol jams can be instantly cleared by the shooter himself,* while most revolver jams will so thoroughly disable the gun that it won't fire until it has been attended to by a gunsmith. A high primer on a cartridge can tie a revolver's cylinder up so tight that it not only won't rotate to permit fir-ing, but may require an armorer to pound the cylinder out of the frame with a rubber mallet. If an auto-pistol cartridge has a high primer, the cyclic action of the slide driving the cartridge into the firing chamber will usually slap the primer into its pocket where it belongs, allowing the cartridge to be fired.

*Constant jamming that gave police autoloaders bad reputation is largely a thing of the past. These 3 police 9mm. autos give same or bet-ter reliability than revolver, one reason being their wide open ejection ports. L to R: Beretta 92F, Ruger P-85, SIG-Sauer P-225.*

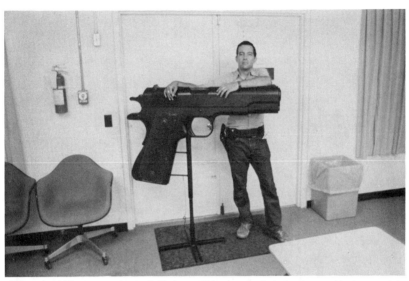

*Officer should learn operation and takedown of his auto pistol. Author poses with giant mockup of Colt .45 auto used in pistol training at Federal Law Enforcement Training Center. 1981 photo courtesy FLETC.*

The most common revolver jam, a spent cartridge casing jammed under the ejector star of a Smith & Wesson, normally takes the average officer some ten seconds to clear, minimum, and requires special tools like the Persuader IV DeJammer if it is to be rectified any quicker. The worst malfunction of an auto pistol, the double feed due to extraction failure, can be cleared by the average officer with training in as little as five to six seconds.

A cartridge that is not seated fully in its firing chamber can prevent a revolver *or* an auto pistol from firing. With the revolver, one must slap the cylinder out, press forcibly down on the heads of all six cartridges, then close the cylinder and try again. With the auto, one simply slaps the back of the slide smartly with the heel of the support hand, forcing the round into the chamber, and one is instantly ready to fire again.

*Fast ammo change capability.* Rather than reloading speed, we're talking here about changing the type of ammo in the weapon immediately prior to an unusual situation. Sgt. Larry Henderson of Houston PD carried an authorized SIG P-220 .45 auto on duty, with Winchester Silvertips in the gun and a clip of the same ammo in his mag pouch, plus a magazine of Speer 200-grain hollowpoints. His experience indicated the Silvertip would have the least penetration, a major concern in his urban area.

*Double action auto is ideal for cold weather, irrespective of whether gloves are worn. Cold, numb hands lose control of revolver triggers or cocked autos, gloved hand can reduce sensation enough to cause accidental discharge with cocked and locked auto and glove can block trigger return inside trigger guard of service revolver after first shot. DA auto, like author's SIG P-220 .45, shown, eliminates all these problems in all weather service.*

*Training in winter weather will show the officers advantages of double action auto pistols. Here author draws a Bren Ten in DA mode during bitter January qualification in New Hampshire.*

Faced with a situation of a fleeing car containing suspects believed to be armed, Sgt. Henderson drove with one hand, using the other to exchange magazines and shoved in seven Speers, which his tests showed would work much better on auto tires than the Silvertips. The chambered Silvertip went into the tire with no immediate effect, but the following Speers did deflate it almost immediately. The vehicle came to a stop a short distance from the point of the shooting, and by the time Henderson emerged to arrest the now-quiescent suspects, he had fully reloaded with Silvertips, a Speer still in the chamber. He believes the life-threatening pursuit might have gone on considerably longer without the ability to instantly change ammo to suit immediate police needs.

As early as 1972, this writer had recommended that the officer with an auto pistol carry one reserve magazine of KTW armor-piercing ammo, on the theory that it might be needed in an unusual situation, and that after a drawn-out gun battle in which other ammo was depleted and the suspect(s) still active, it was safe to assume that the perpetrators were either wearing armor, or by now behind firm cover. Sgt. Evan Marshall, the noted Detroit PD officer survival authority, subsequently and enthusiastically pushed the same concept, and now carries one magazine of exotic armor-piercing ammo along with a spare clip of Silvertips to back up the Silvertips in his double-action 9mm. duty pistol.

This writer generally carries 230-grain hardball to back up the easy-opening hollowpoints in his .45 auto even off duty, and with the 9mm., is likely to carry Federal hollowpoints in the weapon and either 123-grain hardball or BAT rounds in the auxiliary magazine. While teaching in Venezuela, a country where police officers are far more likely to be involved in firefights than in the U.S., he discovered that it was a common practice among the most experienced and knowledgeable officers to load their ubiquitous Browning 9mm. service autos with BAT loads (which combine great shock power with excellent tactical penetration) and back them up with one or two clips of the government arsenal's steel-bullet Cavim armor piercing. While Cavim-type ammo is altogether too penetrative for anything but a special purpose load in the U.S., it is indicated in traffic-choked Caracas since a high proportion of police gunfights there involve multiple, heavily armed perpetrators hiding in or behind cars. After a short time carrying a .45 in that city, the writer had seen enough firefight reports to switch to 9mm. BAT/Cavim loading concept as well.

Extended magazines of proven reliability and 20-round capacity exist for Smith & Wesson, Beretta, Browning and SIG-Sauer 9mm. auto pistols. While too bulky for routine holster carry, a properly designed magazine pouch can carry them very comfortably on duty and even for concealed carry. If loaded with the proper ammunition, they give an officer who has had warning of an encounter time to execute a tactical reload and, if the appropriate ammo is contained in the extended magazine, make his entry to the danger scene armed with a weapon that fires 20 instead of 12 to 16 rounds. This can be a confidence builder as well as a tactical advantage.

*Author demonstrates rapid fire technique with 20-rd. magazine. Two bottom fingers of support hand curl around extended portion of SIG P-226's magazine, pulling back toward body: added leverage locks muzzle on target during rapid fire.*

(Two points should be noted here on extended magazines. First, the only ones that have been found totally trustworthy are those made by the gun companies themselves for their own models, not aftermarket designs from the "cottage industry"; and second, the extended butt of the pistol with long mag inserted creates a leverage point that allows a skilled martial artist to more easily disarm an officer so equipped if a physical conflict should occur at contact distance. Clearly, the extended magazine should only be employed in a situation where there is no other option but gunfire, since it compromises the officer's weapon retention ability in hand-to-hand arrest situations.)

It should also be noted that the extended magazine allows highly advanced shooters to take a low, leverage-controlling firing hold that permits a phenomenal submachine gun-like rate of accurate, controlled fire that would not be possible with any handgun of "normal" grip length. While this advantage in shooting capability should probably be forbidden in intra-departmental tests of handgun skill for badges or salary bonuses for proven competence à la LAPD, it is worth considering by those officers who carry such weapons, and may one day have to use them in an arena in which the only rules are whether or not you were legal, and the only criterion for victory was whether or not you survived.

There is documented reason to believe that, in at least some cases, the sight of the auto pistol in the officer's hand or holster may engender more fear and compliance on the part of certain potentially dangerous suspects. Every department that uses the .45 auto can tell you of cases where criminals surrendered at the point of that gun, because they had been cowed by old wive's tales that a "bullet from a .45 will rip your arm clean off", as one television character put it. The classic example was the suspect who led El Monte, CA, patrolmen on a foot pursuit. Cornered, he spun toward the officers and started to reach for the pistol in his belt. Suddenly, he looked at their issue Colt automatics and raised his empty hands, shouting, "No *fair!* You bastards got forty-*fives!*"

This effect is a sometime thing. First, it presumes that the offender learned from military training or street scuttlebutt the rumor that .45 automatics are much more powerful than they actually are. Many of today's street punks have no access to military training or to role models so trained. Second, as officer survival expert John Farnam has observed, many criminals believe they know the law better than the arresting officer and are convinced that the officer won't dare shoot at him for fear of disciplinary action or lawsuits. No such criminal fears the most powerful gun if he doesn't believe the officer is going to fire it at him.

Oddly enough, this aspect of deterrence as a function of the type of gun translates more toward the armed private citizen's use of threatened deadly force against criminal suspects, and it goes the other way. I advise civilian students that the revolver in *their* hand might well be more intimidating to a criminal than an auto pistol. The reason is that when you see an auto pistol from the business end, you see merely the muzzle of a gun. When you look at a revolver from the same perspective, you can see the bullets in the firing chambers. A criminal confronted with this sight knows that Joe Citizen's gun *is loaded.* Bullets are poised to be launched through his own personal body if he, the criminal suspect, does not surrender to the householder and wait for the police. With the revolver, it is clear that the civilian is not bluffing with Grand-dad's empty World War II souvenir automatic.

This is a factor for civilians to consider, because criminals perceive their victims as too soft to effectively fight them. Therefore, the civilian who presumes to take a criminal at gunpoint needs every edge he can get to reinforce his position.

This is not necessarily true for most police officers. Unless the officer comes across as a wimp, the criminal bloody well knows that the cop is as streetwise as he himself and at least as dangerous when attacked. He also knows that all policemen carry loaded guns, so the question of running a bluff is less a factor.

Indeed, there is evidence to suggest that certain criminals are particularly respectful of police officers who are armed with automatics, since they see that type of gun as a badge of combat shooting expertise. Officer survival authority and former police chief Al Pickles writes about one hard-core, gun-carrying criminal who was debriefed by officers. The thug explained that when sizing up an officer, he always looked to his holster. A standard revolver with factory-furnished grips told him that this officer didn't care much about shooting, was probably a mediocre shot and a slow draw, and didn't have a lot of survival awareness. He rated such cops easy to take if he wanted to challenge them.

He was more leery of an officer whose revolver wore custom grips, like Hogue or Pachmayr. This told him that the officer was probably "into" guns to some degree, therefore probably faster and deadlier than the average cop, and probably had gunfight survival closer to the forefront of his mind. The suspect implied that he was more reluctant to cross such an officer.

The suspect indicated that he was particularly put off by cops who carried automatics; here, he believed, was an officer he was unlikely to outgun, an officer who might possibly shoot him several times if he faced him off.

The worst, the suspect said, the one officer he absolutely would not pull a gun on, was the cop who carried a .45 automatic cocked and locked. The suspect perceived himself extremely knowledgeable and expert on firearms and himself carried a cocked and locked .45 auto. He said that gun was the mark of the master gunfighter, and he would avoid at all costs tangling with such an officer.

Part of this may have been the suspect's exaggerated self-esteem and belief in his own skills ("I carry a .45 auto and consider myself a master gunfighter; ergo, anyone else who carries one is probably also a master gunfighter"). Yet it cannot be written off entirely. Any police firearms instructor can tell you of looking at an officer carrying an unmodified .38 in a cheap holster, perhaps backed with ammo in obsolete dump pouches, and making Barney Fife jokes. If this is the low level of respect gun-wise cops hold for brother officers who carry "lowest common denominator" equipment, is it so hard to believe that highly dangerous, streetwise criminals would have the exact same reaction?

A more measurable factor with officers who carry semiautomatic duty handguns is *enhanced individual officer confidence.* In his excellent book about police work, "Target Blue", former deputy NYPD Commissioner Robert Daley commented that while the gun and the badge are the two most definable symbols of the job, the gun is the more psychologically significant of the two. A plainclothesman can leave his badge in its hidden folder, but is still identified by the gun on his hip when he takes his coat off, yet the officer on punitive transfer or light duty who wears badge and uniform but no gun becomes the target of ridicule and scorn by brother officers.

Thus, the gun becomes the repository of part of the officer's occupational self-image. I found that in departments like LAPD where each officer has a very strong spit and polished self image and likes to look good and present himself well, almost every service revolver would sport custom grips designed to best fit the officer's hand. (Interestingly, LAPD is also one of the few police departments with the laudable practice of giving every officer bonus pay if he shoots a high score at monthly firearms qualification). When I did work for the Police Benevolent Association in New York City, I noticed that in low-action precincts ("C-houses") the average cop would have worn-out, factory-standard grips on his service revolver, but in a heavy-action "A-House", a majority of the officers' revolvers would sport custom grips or at least grip adapters. Part of it was that officers who saw themselves most in danger wanted logically to be more effective fighters if they had to use deadly force in self-defense, but there was also the unspoken feeling among many brother officers that a cop who didn't bother to fit the gun to his hand was a guy who might just be hiding psychologically from the danger the brother officers all perceived themselves as facing.

What, then, of the auto pistol? In many departments, only SWAT members are issued semiautomatics. The gun thus became the badge of the high achiever, the supercop, the way in one department the leather patrol jacket became the mark of the elite because its use was authorized only for crack Mounted and Tactical Patrol Force officers.

The psychological aspect is the least of it. The officer who perceives himself facing highly dangerous criminal types may know *intellectually* that the autoloading pistol gives him a fight-winning advantage, and the confidence he feels when he straps one on is very real. As will be seen elsewhere in this book, New Jersey troopers knew that "If the bad guys could get Phil Lamonico, they could get any of us", and they perceived that their super-trooper had been killed by the robbers only because they had him outgunned with high-capacity 9mm. autos. Many troopers had already decided to flagrantly violate department rules by carrying privately owned high-capacity 9mm.s as concealed backup guns. The department's issuance of the nine-shot HK P7 autoloader greatly bolstered the overall confidence of the entire patrol force.

Let us go back to the first critical advantage of the auto pistol, its propensity to allow its user to deliver better hit potential in rapid combat fire. Unquestionably, on a revolver department, the officer who qualifies Expert feels more confident than his partner, who barely qualifies at the lowly Marksman level. An officer who has switched to the easy shooting semiautomatic and found himself shooting Expert or even Master scores feels that same boost in confidence. He and his equipment are one, and it's not that the gun lets him shoot Expert for the first time, it's that *he* can finally shoot Expert.

The required firearms qualification is the only opportunity the average officer has to compare his skill and performance with a recognized regional or national standard. Things like arrest ratio, activity of contact, and conviction rate are all functions of society, demographics, local court practices, and the time and location of shift assignments at least as much as they are avatars of the officer's own ability to do his job. But the ability to fire on a recognized pistol qualification course is a benchmark of the officer's skill. When we talk the 25% street hit potential of the revolver versus the 65% street hit potential of the double-action service automatic, *we are talking a 160% performance increase.* This is a quantum leap. An officer who improved his arrest rate 160% above the average would doubtless be named "officer of the month" at his station. Likewise, the officer who shoots higher with his new auto than he did with his old revolver feels well-deserved elation and confidence: he can do his job better, and he is safer. This is the bottom line of the confidence factor.

*Reasonable modifications should be allowed on privately owned, department approved service pistols. This Beretta 92 Compact improved owner's performance greatly after high-visibility Millett sights were installed by gunsmith Russ Jefferson.*

Obviously, if the officer has not been trained, or his auto pistol and ammo have been poorly selected and jam frequently, the opposite effect on confidence will take place. Suffice to say that, properly introduced, the auto pistol should enhance the officer's confidence in his own safety and survival skills, a confidence that can easily spread to his own self-image and dedication to his job.

*Thus, the secondary advantages to authorizing or adopting the semi-automatic police service pistol are better night-shooting characteristics, superior adaptability to plainclothes wear by off-duty personnel and detectives, more relevant and court-defensible training, ease of repair, ease of malfunction clearance and, in some instances, enhanced confidence of the officers and enhanced deterrent effect when the officers draw their guns on hardened criminal suspects.*

We have discussed many of the auto pistol's strong points. What about the weak points? They certainly exist, and should be addressed in any discussion of the police autoloader — partly to give a balanced view to the decision makers, and partly to consider ways of compensating for the design's shortcomings. We shall address that issue next.

*The double tap, a rapid two-shot burst with first shot aimed and second hammered immediately after the first, works best with auto pistols and is ideal for use with 9mm.s. Here Ayoob's Ruger P-85 is caught by hi-speed camera in mid-cycle after second shot: one casing is above ejection port, the other falling just in front of pistol, showing speed of delivery . . . yet muzzle is still level on target, where both bullets struck center 4" apart at 7 yards.*

*Double tap training, LFI style. Relay 1 shooters fire double tap as relay two observes with "coach and pupil" method . . .*

*. . . and after each double tap, observer touches shooter on back to show where each hit went. This is because recoil obscures view of which bullet hit where, especially if student is watching his sights as trained.*

# AUTO PISTOL SHORTCOMINGS
# AND HOW TO CORRECT THEM

The autoloader is by no means without its weak points. These include: a historical tendency to jam more often than revolvers, a tendency in some designs to be more prone to accidental discharge than revolvers, design features that make it less suitable for barricade shooting than revolvers, inability to function reliably with certain types of cartridges, unintentional disassembly in some models, and a tendency for some models to release their magazines unintentionally. Each of these problems, where they exist, can be rectified; with knowledgeable police policy making, they can be prevented from ever happening.

*Historically, auto pistols jam more often than revolvers.* Anyone who has taken a course at Gunsite Ranch, Chapman Academy, John Farnam's school, or Lethal Force Institute has seen revolvers on the line with autos, and has noticed that for some students, the auto pistols seemed disproportionately more likely to malfunction. Facts are facts. Normally, however, the instructors at those schools will show you how to make your own automatics virtually malfunction-free, as theirs are.

First, *select or authorize only those handguns with good performance records.* The Heckler and Koch P7 is perhaps the most jam-free handgun made, including revolvers. In the early 1980s this writer received sample #51136 from the HK headquarters. We had been told that if the gas ports clogged, the weapon would cease to function. Wanting to find out how many rounds it would take for this to happen, I assigned this gun as a "loaner" for the range, to be used by students whose own guns had failed or who wanted to try an auto instead of a revolver. Since we knew that the aluminum jackets of then-current first and second generation Silvertip ammo were flaking off and clogging P7 gas systems, and since we knew that lead reloads would do the same, we stipulated that only copper-jacketed round-nose or hollowpoint ammo be used in the gun. Currently Silvertip, by the way, performs superbly in P7 pistols. Many students fired their entire 500 rounds of the course with this pistol. There was one more stipulation, however: *students and instructors were not to clean the gun!* It was to be wiped down on the outside to prevent rust from sweaty handling, and the slide and muzzle area could be oiled, but the pistol was not to be disassembled, nor were the students even to run a brush down the bore.

At around the two thousandth shot, the slide operation became noticeably rough. Nonetheless, the pistol would still feed and fire without a hitch. Shortly before the 4,500th cartridge was fired without cleaning, we observed two failures of the slide to lock open on an empty magazine. Knowing that this was the first warning of a gas port sufficiently clogged to impair functioning, we called off the test at that time and turned the pistol over to HK-trained armorer Rick Devoid. The disassembly of the pistol, for the first time in 4,500 rounds, was photographed.

*This is the interior of author's test HK P7 after it fired more than 4,000 factory rounds including hollowpoint without a single malfunction, **without being stripped or cleaned**. Author considers P7 the most reliable police handgun ever made, finds performance of test gun typical of the great many he has seen and monitored in police service.*

Unburned flakes of powder were noted throughout the parts. Carbon buildup resembled an engine that needed a valve job. *Yet there had never been a single failure of the pistol to fire, eject the shell, rechamber, and fire again!*

This level of reliability is phenomenal. I can think of no revolver I would expect to still be firing after 4,500 rounds without cleaning. In a recent test by the Federal Law Enforcement Training Center using mixed .38 Special +P, +P+, and .357 ammo, all specimens of the medium-frame .357 Magnum revolver submitted for testing by the leading manufacturer were jamming or indeed had broken down by the time that number of rounds had been fired. It should be noted that no breakages occurred in the HK. Furthermore, operating pressures for the 9mm. Parabellum cartridge it fired were around 32,000 Copper Units of Pressure, about the same as .357 Magnum and considerably more than even the hottest .38 Special loads.

In my opinion, the P7 has set a new standard for handgun reliability, revolver *or* autoloader. Yet there are other highly reliable autoloaders on the market.

Smith & Wesson's introduction of the three-digit model number pistols circa 1980 marked the third generation of S&W 9mm., auto development. The first generation model 39 and the second generation model 39-2 and model 59 were flawed weapons. Even after the weak, breakable barrel bushings and strangely stepped feed ramp of the first generation guns were corrected, the pistol still had the tendency to jam more than it should, particularly if it was not well-lubricated. Dropped on the muzzle without the safety on, the gun was likely to go off. All these problems were cured in the third generation: after thirty years, Smith & Wesson had finally figured out how to build a centerfire auto pistol. These guns in 9mm., include models 439 (aluminum frame, blue or nickel, 8-shot); 539 (chrome molybdenum steel frame, 8-shot, blue or nickel), 639 (stainless steel 8-shot), 459 (14-shot aluminum frame, blue or nickel), 559 (steel frame 14-shot, blue or nickel), 659 (stainless steel 14-shot), 469 (compact aluminum frame 12-shot, blue), and 669 (compact 12-shot, stainless slide and hard-chromed aluminum frame). For brevity, these guns will henceforth be referred to as "3D", standing for three-digit model number and also for third generation of manufacture/design.

3D S&W 9mm.s are extremely reliable guns. Oddly enough, the best seem to be the little 469 and 669, which are also the most accurate. It could be that the lighter slide mass of the smaller gun is more forgiving of friction when the gun must cycle while dirty. The "ball and bushing" barrel design of the short pistols seems to provide better lockup than the bigger military service style S&W automatics. This is probably the only instance in handgun manufacturing history where a compact, short-barrelled model variation proved to be more accurate than its full-sized, long-barrel parent gun. American police were quick to recognize this, since numerous small police departments adopted the 469 and 669 as issue handguns for uniform duty as well as plainclothes wear.

The same firm's model 645 has proven to be a phenomenally reliable .45 automatic. Straight-line feed plus factory "throating", or bevelling of the feed ramp and chamber mouth, allow virtually all hollowpoint bullets to feed with aplomb. According to S&W researcher Tom

Campbell, this is the only production auto pistol in the history of the world to be test-fired — every single sample — with 48 rounds of different ammunition. Before it leaves the factory in Springfield, MA, each 645 is supposed to fire six rounds of 185-grain target semiwadcutter (perhaps the toughest load for the average .45 auto to cycle), 6 rounds of GI "hardball", and three dozen rounds of assorted hollowpoints.

Most 645s will perform the cute, if arguably meaningless, trick of feeding empty shell casings when hand-cycled from the magazine. One sample I tested would fire full wadcutter .45 cartridges, loaded flush with the case mouth for shooting "bowling pin matches" with a .45 ACP revolver, and never failed to cycle and discharge.

*Even with DA auto like this Smith 645, hammer is always cocked after first shot, creating danger of accidental discharge under stress. Training should indoctrinate the officer to flip the decocking/safety lever above thumb to return to DA mode and prevent accidental discharge in high-stress moments after firing in line of duty.*

I suspect that the 645 is the pistol that will "make" the .45 auto in law enforcement in the U.S.: it's stainless, it says "Smith & Wesson" on it, it is extremely reliable, and it feeds the best anti-personnel ammo.

Another brand with a proven reputation for reliability in the police service is the SIG-Sauer. Huntington Beach, California, police adopted this gun when Browning was still importing it as their "BDA", and stayed with it after the designation was changed to "SIG-Sauer P-220". In .45 ACP, this weapon served HBPD so well that numerous California law enforcement agencies followed their lead and adopted it. Perhaps more agencies have gone to the same firm's P-226, a 16-shot 9mm. Designed so that the fat staggered magazine is contained in a grip-frame that is trim and comfortable to grasp, the P-226 is very controllable and very accurate. Like the S&W 9mm.s, it can be reloaded with a very functional 20-round magazine. So outfitted, and not pausing to reload, it is possible to shoot the FBI Tactical Revolver Course with this gun in one-fourth to one-fifth of the standard time limits, with a high qualifying score and using full-power hollowpoint 9mm. ammunition.

Beretta has long had a reputation as one of the best builders of auto pistols. Their Jetfire is the most reliable .25 auto ever made, and their model 84 .380 is more reliable and accurate than any gun of its caliber, including the vaunted Walther. Unfortunately, this writer has seen numerous malfunctions with the model 92 series, the pistol adopted by the U.S. Government in 1984 to replace the 1911 Colt .45 auto, a bid that brought lawsuits from Smith and Wesson. I suspect that in modifying the design to fit the U.S. Government JSSAP (Joint Services Small Arms Project) specifications, certain mistakes were made that have been rectified in subsequent production. Suffice to say that many police departments are happy with it, from Los Angeles to the State Police agencies of Wyoming and Connecticut. By 1987, Beretta had its model 92 production quality up to the standards of their other weapons, which make it a fine gun indeed.

LAPD officers, given their choice between the Beretta and the S&W and buying their sidearms out of their own pockets, chose Berettas by more than four to one. A survey of the Las Vegas Metro Police officers, who had long been issued S&W 9mm. 15-shot pistols, showed an overwhelming preference for the Beretta after the cops had tested both side by side.

The first automatic to be accepted in the police service in the U.S. was the Colt. It is not widely known that NYPD became the first big department to issue automatics when, shortly after the turn of the century, they ordered a large number of Colt m/1903 Pocket Pistols. It was quickly decided that the officers would be better off with revolvers.

Military police have used the Colt pattern .45 automatic since 1911, and the legendary Texas Rangers adopted it almost immediately as their unofficial "standard weapon". When Jeff Cooper led the "renaissance of the .45 auto" in the 1950s and 1960s, this was the pistol that gunwise officers pleaded with their chiefs for permission to carry. It offered 8 shots instead of 6 and shock power far beyond that of the 158-grain round-nose lead bullet that was standard for .38 Special service revolvers of the period; it was fast to reload, and it shot surprisingly well once you learned modern combat shooting techniques.

The .45 auto was the first classic SWAT handgun, partly because LAPD perceived the Special Weapons and Tactics Unit as a small infantry team infiltrating the enemy's territory and, if necessary, destroying them there. Training with the military, they naturally came away with military guns: the AR-15 and M-16 rifle, the same bolt-action scoped .308 the services were using for sniper rifles in the early 70s, and, of course, the GI .45 automatic.

*Author's Colt .38 automatic customized by Jim Clark has stippling on front strap. This after-market feature in no way interferes with reliability, but gives gun steadier hold in firing and a more secure purchase to aid weapon retention in a struggle for the weapon.*

*Ray Chapman shot his way to World Combat Championship with Colt .45 auto, still considers it an ideal police sidearm. He converted his department to that gun when working as a full time cop in the 60s. Photo courtesy Silver Image.*

It remains an excellent choice of police weapon, but only in expert hands. It is generally accepted that a double-action autoloader is safer for gunpoint and arrest situations than is a pistol like the single-action Colt, which must be cocked before it can fire.

More to the point, it is not totally reliable with hollowpoint anti-personnel ammunition in all its forms. The average Colt .45 autoloader is designed by the factory to feed only "GI hardball", the round-nose, copper-jacketed 230-grain bullet. The Remington 185-grain jacketed hollowpoint .45 police load has the same feeding characteristics, and will generally cycle 100% through any .45 auto that feeds hardball to the same standard of reliability.

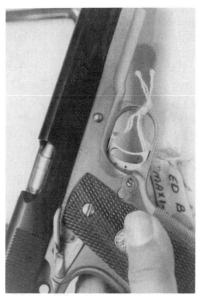

*Even the best pistols can malfunction with poor quality or reloaded ammunition. This Eddie Brown Custom Colt .45 competition auto jammed on lead semiwadcutter load, a round not suitable for the police service autoloader.*

*Some autoloaders will not feed all popular police loads as manufactured. This particular Colt Lightweight Officer's Model .45 was flawless with hardball and Remington hollowpoint, but would not feed other hollowpoints without the feed ramp being throated by armorer.*

Later model Colts, designed expressly for the police service, are "factory throated" for better feeding of a wide variety of police-style hollowpoints. These guns include the blue steel Combat Government and stainless steel Government models. My stainless Government Mk IV Series '80 fired approximately 4,000 rounds of hardball, hollowpoints, and lead bullet handloads with fewer than ten malfunctions, all of which could be traced to bad reload ammo or an extremely weak hold on the gun. Shortly after the 4,000th round, "wiring" occurred in the slide rails on the frame, that is, a roughening of the surface. This was polished out and the gun continued to be reliable with hollowpoints, firing some 1,000 Federal, Remington, and Super Vel hollowpoints without further malfunction. I have trusted, and would trust, this pistol with my life. I would not feel the same way about the average 1911 or Government Model pistol, out of the factory box and loaded with hollowpoints. Once "throated" and tested by a custom gunsmith, however, any good specimen of the Colt .45 auto will be reliable enough to stake your life on with most hollowpoints.

The Star PD, once the issue handgun for Indiana State Police narcotics' detectives and extremely popular among off-duty cops in hot climates like Miami's, is also an extremely reliable gun. The pistol is fitted with a rubber recoil buffer that, since it is slightly "chewed" by the steely impact of the slide mechanism every time the gun fires, needs replacement every 500 to 750 rounds, a routine as easy as cleaning the service revolver. Unfortunately, Star never mentioned this in their handout material with the pistol, and some people whose PD pistols jammed on shredded rubber when 2,000 or more rounds had been fired came to feel that the gun "would start jamming after you shot it some". Properly maintained, the PD is a thoroughly reliable handgun, especially with .45 hollowpoints.

The point is, numerous autoloading pistols exist that have proven themselves more than reliable enough for the rigors of police service. The above-named guns — HK P7s, 3D Smith & Wessons, SIG-Sauers, 645s, Colt Stainless and Combat Government Models — will feed every bit as reliably as revolvers once they have been broken in. It is generally accepted that any semiautomatic pistol, due to the long bearing surfaces where the slide contacts the frame, needs to be "shot in" with some 200 rounds of ammunition to "seat the parts", in the sense of the slow 500 first miles on a new car's engine to allow the components to break in smoothly with one another. It is significant that guns like the HK, SIG, and Colt stainless usually won't jam their first 200 rounds, either; mine haven't. In any case, well over 200 rounds will be fired by the officers during their familiarization and qualification period before they ever carry the gun on the job.

*Some autoloading pistols are more prone to accidental discharge than revolvers.* The revolver is simple to handle and inspect: you swing out the cylinder and check if there are cartridges in the chambers or not. The auto pistol requires that you first remove the magazine, and then operate the slide to clear the live round out of the firing chamber. Something can go wrong at this stage if you are careless.

If the gun has been fired a lot without cleaning, carbon buildup on the back of the chambered cartridge can look black enough to create the visual illusion of an empty chamber. When the slide is back enough to allow you to look into the ejection port, it can cast a shadow over the chamber and make it look empty when it isn't. This is most likely to happen with strong overhead light: high noon at the firing range or at night when the intense artificial beam of the rangemaster's flashlight is played on the gun, creating a very stark light and shadow effect.

Three contemporary police service autos have slides that are cut away in this area to prevent such problems: the Beretta 92 series, the Ruger P-85 and the SIG-Sauers. With other autoloaders, the officers should be encouraged to lock their slides back when they unload their weapons, and "check by sight and feel". By this I mean that while the dominant hand firmly holds the gun, the little finger of the weak hand — the narrowest of the ten digits — actually probes the magazine well inside the grip frame to make sure the magazine has fallen clear, and actually probes the firing chamber via the ejection port to make sure that no cartridge has been left there. The only popular police service automatic the latter is not possible with is the HK P7; once the slide is back, the small ejection port is so far back from the breech area of the barrel that no finger on the average adult male hand can reach the port. The solution is for the instructor to insert a Persuader IV DeJammer, a Bic Stik pen, or something similar down the barrel until it protrudes in the area visible through the ejection port of the slide, proving that no round is still in the chamber.

Certain autoloading pistols can accidentally discharge if dropped on the muzzle or hammer area, particularly the former. The first two generations of Smith & Wesson autoloading 9mm.s were notorious for this. A firing pin lock on the third generation guns has solved the problem.

*Accidental discharges due to dropping, a real concern with older generation autos, is not present in contemporary service pistols. Shown is the firing pin lock on the Series '80 Colt police automatics. Photo courtesy Colt Firearms.*

With the earlier Colt 1911-style .45 automatics (Government model, Commanders, Gold Cups, Combat Elites, etc.), it is theoretically possible for the gun to AD (accidentally discharge) from being dropped only if it falls from a height of ten feet or more onto a surface as hard as concrete. However, this assumes that the gun is in the same condition as it left the factory. A worn firing pin spring can allow the inertia-operated firing pin to bounce forward far enough and hard enough to accidentally discharge from a much shorter drop on the muzzle.

If the gun falls onto the hammer area with the hammer down or in the half-cocked position, the 1911 pattern pistol may accidentally discharge if it does not have a series '80 firing pin safety. As the firing pin bounces backward and strikes the down hammer, it rebounds with enough force to possibly fire the weapon. If it lands on the half-cocked hammer, the half-cock notch can break and drive the hammer a fraction of an inch forward under the still-captured pressure of the Colt pistol's very powerful mainspring. It will now hit with enough force to very possibly fire the gun, whose muzzle is now pointing up.

This is why a single-action, outside-hammer pistol like the Colt 1911 series or the Browning Hi-Power **should never be carried with hammer all the way down *or* on half cock with a live round in the firing chamber.** Such guns should be carried ONLY in "Condition One", that is, with the hammer cocked, live round in chamber and full magazine in place, and manual safety in the "on safe" position. Now, if the gun should fall, only the firing pin's own inertia has to be contended with, not the added force of the hammer's inadvertent blow to the firing pin which, after all, is what makes it go off in the first place when you pull the trigger.

The Series '80 design by Colt solves this problem; a separate mechanism locks the firing pin and allows it to move forward *only* when the trigger has been pulled. Many officers still carry older model Colts and Brownings. Those who do are cautioned to make sure they have full-power firing pin springs in place, to reduce the likelihood of "inertia firing". Still, the Series '80 design in the Colt service automatic and the 3D configuration in the Smith & Wesson service automatic, are the most positive guarantees against an accidental discharge. With the HK P7, if the grip squeeze-cocker has not been activated, it is physically impossible for the pistol to discharge due to being dropped or similar impact. Of course, all guns should be periodically checked to make sure that the safety devices function properly. It has been rumored that one agency found that metal fatigue in a few of their P7's caused the firing pin blocking mechanism to be compromised after some 10,000 rounds.

Dropped guns, and chamber-loaded guns that were thought to be unloaded, have just been dealt with. These are two of the major profiles seen when police service automatics fire accidentally. The third pattern is the unintentional discharge of a pistol held in the officer's hand, and already cocked, when a blow or sudden sound causes a startled reflex that triggers the gun.

Examples of this have in fact occurred. They include the following:

— Vancouver, Washington. A plainclothes officer makes an arrest at the point of his cocked Colt .45 auto, the safety off. The suspect jumps him and struggles for the gun. The officer yells for a nearby uniformed officer to assist him. In the struggle, the trigger is depressed and the cocked gun fires. The bullet strikes in the face the uniformed officer who is racing to the narc's aid, and he is killed instantly.

— Miami, Florida. While battering down the entrance of a rock house, a SWAT commander's elbow is struck violently by a suddenly opening door. His hand closes reflexively on his HK P7 automatic, which fires, sending a bullet into the left arm of a brother member of the special response team. In turn, the wounded officer's arms reflexively and spasmodically contract, and the sympathetic muscular convulsion causes his trigger finger to close on the shotgun he is holding. The 12-gauge discharges, striking a noncombatant pregnant female, with one pellet going past to strike a young boy. The woman loses one hand; pellets cause the unborn child to be delivered with a permanent club foot.

— Hampton Beach, New Hampshire. A suspect during a felony stop reaches up and grabs the Colt Gold Cup .45 automatic being held by the arresting sergeant. Reflexively, as the suspect tries to pull the gun away, the officer's own hand tightens. Simultaneously, the thumb locks down and wipes the safety into the "fire" position as the trigger finger, extended outside the trigger guard, snaps inward with impact. The resulting shot sends a 200-grain Speer hollowpoint bullet into the lower face of the suspect, resulting in what the medical report calls "avulsion of the lower mandible", that is, the unarmed suspect's lower jaw is shot completely away. After criminal trial for aggravated assault, the sergeant will be found not guilty, but his police career will be poisoned thereafter.

How can these accidental discharges be avoided? Frankly, even staying with double-action revolvers won't keep it from happening. When two adult men struggle for a gun, hundreds of pounds of force are being exerted — approximately a thousand pounds of force, estimates the engineer and world combat pistol champion Ray Chapman — and with that kind of raw power in play, it ceases to matter whether the trigger pull on the gun in question weighs four pounds or fourteen pounds, the difference between cocked and uncocked.

The Vancouver officer might well have been killed if the gun his brother cop and the felon were fighting over had been a double-action service revolver. The blow to the "crazy bone" that triggered the fateful shot from the P7 in Florida might well have triggered any police handgun, double or single action. An officer holding a traditional revolver with his thumb high and his trigger finger outside the guard might, like the Hampton sergeant, have tightened his grip so solidly when the criminal suspect tried to rip his gun away, that even a double-action gun could have fired.

Yet in lawsuits against police, the "cocked-gun argument", with its connotation to the jury of "hair triggers", is so popular that at least one expert witness has almost made a specialty of claiming that the officer's gun was cocked and ergo, his reckless actions made him responsible for a shooting that didn't have to be. One such expert has faced me twice — and lost both times — in cases where he testified the cop had cocked his service revolver, *even though all the evidence showed that the officer had fired double action.*

The simplest way to prevent such an accidental shooting is to issue or authorize only *double-action* autoloading pistols. These require that a long, heavy trigger pull be actuated to fire the first shot.

With any handgun, including the traditional service revolver, the finger should be outside the trigger guard if the officer anticipates having to struggle for the gun. However, logic shows us that if the officer *did* have reason to believe he'd have to struggle for the gun, he would have stayed back on the perimeter of danger and not approached at all. The very fact that the officer is struggling for the gun indicates that he was attacked by someone who took him by surprise.

Face it, folks: when two men struggle over a loaded gun, knowing that if the attacker gets the defender's gun away he's likely to kill him with it, both parties are going to be exerting maximum physical pressure. Whether it's an automatic or a revolver is the least of it. Many police academies now use hand dynamometers to register the hand strength of recruits and in-service personnel, since physiologists believe this measurement is a good clue to overall physical conditioning. On my dynamometer, I can generally on command come within a few pounds of my body weight, 160. I have seen large, powerful men who could exert over two hundred pounds of grip pressure. I find that weak, out of condition, middle-aged females with tiny hands can still exert 50 to 60 pounds of hand strength. Really, the difference between 4 pounds of pressure on a Condition One .45 automatic and 14 pounds of pressure on a 12-pound double-action revolver trigger ceases to be significant.

According to Police Officer Ralph Sorrento, former statistical officer of NYPD's acclaimed Firearms and Tactics Unit, situations occur six times a year in New York when officers shoot men who are struggling with them for their guns. The total number of discharges during struggles is larger; Sorrento had been asked only for the number of situations in which the officers shot the men who were grappling for their weapons. It will be noted that virtually all these incidents involve the double-action .38 revolver that NYPD mandates its officers to carry.

Clearly, then, double-action weapons aren't an answer to the problem by themself. The author recommends a two-pronged approach to preventing accidental discharges during struggles for the police weapon. First, all officers should be trained in the Lindell Method of Handgun Retention, developed for the Kansas City, MO, Police Department by Jim Lindell of the Kansas City Regional Police Training Academy. Lindell's method is by far the strongest and most street-proven method of keeping control of the police service handgun when a suspect attacks the gun in the hand or the holster.

Second, the author recommends that officers be taught to remove the finger from the trigger guard in close physical arrest situations or weapon struggles, not merely by extending the trigger finger straight forward as used to be commonly taught, but with the "LFI method" in which the trigger finger is flexed and placed on the frame of the weapon above as well as outside the trigger guard.

This is the conventional method of holding the index finger off the trigger when entering a danger situation or on the range. Author suggests this technique only for holstering, has found four potentially dangerous problems when it is used in a "ready position."

The LFI ready technique, with the trigger finger crooked, solves all four of the concerns created with the straight finger technique (see text).

As photos will show, this flexed trigger finger position solves at least four potentially lethal problems that are posed when the trigger finger is extended stiffly outside the trigger guard. Those problems are:

1) When extended, the trigger finger is slow to get inside the guard if the officer does in fact have to pull the trigger to save his life or another's.

2) The extended finger can press on the "takedown stud" of the slide release on semiautomatic pistols like the Colt 1911 series, the Browning Hi-Power, or the first two generations of S&W 9mm. automatics. After

the first shot is subsequently fired, the pistol may begin to disassemble itself due to recoil force.

3) When the extended finger comes back toward the trigger, it is held taut for a moment by the front of the trigger guard, and now when it clears, it comes straight back onto the trigger, with impact. This is what caused the shooting in the Hampton Beach case.

4) When the trigger finger is extended alongside the pistol, a suspect who grabs the gun and moves it toward that finger hyperextends it. Now, the whole hand must let go, or the trigger finger will be broken. This hold, finger extended straight forward, is extremely weak for weapon retention.

The LFI "cocked finger" position solves all these problems. The bent trigger finger indexes itself with the fingernail behind the slide release stud on the auto, or on the forward frame screw of the service revolver. Try it as seen in the photos. In this position:

1) The trigger finger can instantly access the trigger if a shot has to be made; there's nothing in the way to stop it.

2) Properly indexed and already touching the frame, the fingertip cannot apply pressure to the takedown stud of vulnerable pistol designs.

3) The finger, when it contacts the trigger, comes straight across it. It never is held taut, and never comes back to the trigger with impact. It simply slides into position, ready to deliver the firing stroke when the officer's mind commands.

4) Being flexed, the finger can almost infinitely resist lateral pressure, long enough to defeat the gun-grab attack and allow the officer to successfully execute the weapon retention technique of his choice.

The bottom line to our discussion is this: **with proper weapon selection and proper training, the police department need have no greater number of accidental discharges than it experienced with revolvers if the department changes to well designed service semiautomatics.**

Another concern with police autoloaders is that *autoloaders are not as amenable as revolvers to being fired from a position behind barricade cover.* It is understood that the survival-oriented officer will seek hard cover as soon as a firefight threatens, and will, if necessary, fire from that position.

Revolvers work better from behind barricade cover. When the service automatic is fired while held next to a corner of a wall, the recoiling slide can contact the barricade surface and, with friction or actual blocking, keep the weapon from cycling its next cartridge. If fired around the left side of a wall, since most auto pistols eject to the right, an auto pistol held upright and close to the wall can eject the shell against the barricade surface hard enough to cause the spent casing to bounce back into the pistol's action in mid-cycle, jamming the weapon. One Las Vegas police sergeant told the author that such an incident occurred during one of the first shootouts LVPD engaged in after adopting the Smith & Wesson model 59 as the standard service pistol for the department. The officer reportedly fired around a left side wall, and the spent shell bounced into the open chamber and jammed the slide mechanism. Fortunately, no officers were hurt as a result of this reported incident, and the incident itself was not recorded in LVPD records.

*"Roll-out position," here supervised by famed police survival instructor John Farnam, keeps officer and gun back and clear of barricade, is one solution to problem of autos jamming from contact with barricade. However, roll-out position exposes more of body from behind one's cover.*

*When firing from barricade in conventional positions, care must be taken that slide does not contact the wall or resulting friction can jam pistol.*

*Author uses roll-out technique while winning "1st class A" at Paladin combat shoot in Miami. Pistol is Colt .45 duty auto drawn from concealed carry.*

Techniques exist to prevent this problem. It should be noted at the outset that the very real problem will not usually manifest itself on the police training range, where the simulated barricades are simply 4x6 pieces of wood. On the police shooting course, the spent shells will clear. When fired from an actual barricade like the side of a building, shells can in fact bounce back into the action and jam the gun.

Jim Cirillo, an NYPD Stakeout Squad officer and former firearms instructor for that department, developed a firing technique for right-handed officers to shoot from a left-side wall without switching the hand-gun between hands. The gun was simply turned 45° sideways when coming up on the weak side. When this "Cirillo cant" is applied to the auto pistol on the left side of the barricade by a left OR right handed officer, it keeps the slide clear of jamming against the barricade, and the ejection arc of the spent casings now safely travels straight up and over the officer's head. It is suggested at the Lethal Force Institute that officers with auto pistols use the 45° cant even on the strong side to prevent slide contact with the wall. The added exposure of the body is insignificant, and the overall shooting posture is strengthened. Even if the officer should be shooting the German Walther P-5, the one centerfire automatic that ejects to the left, he is still automatically fail-safed by this technique.

*On left wall, spent casing can be bounced back into ejection port, jamming gun. This "Cirillo rotation" not only keeps slide clear of wall, but moves ejection arc upward, clearing the barricade and preventing bounce-back jams.*

*Even on right side of barricade, Cirillo rotation guarantees that slide will not be impeded by contact with barricade. Pistol is S&W 645.*

*Police Chief Cameron Harbison demonstrates proper barricade position from inside cruisier. Note that his S&W 669 9mm. is canted slightly to prevent jams due to slide or spent casing contact with door frame.*

Some semiautomatic pistols will not feed any cartridge but full metal jacket, round-nosed, "GI hardball". In the early days of the police experience with autoloaders, this was a real problem. For more than a decade, however, the answers have been known among the better-informed police firearms instructors.

First, one can have guns that will feed proper hollowpoint police ammunition. These include such "factory throated" guns as the Smith & Wesson 645 and 3D automatics in .45 ACP and 9mm. respectively, the stainless Colt Government Mk IV and Combat Government .45s in blue steel, the HK P7, and the SIG pistol series, as well as the Star PD combat .45 autoloader.

If the department's weapons policy is such that the exact models cannot be dictated by command, then it is most certainly Command's prerogative to specify what cartridges will be carried on duty. Court decisions from California have held that the issuing authority has the right and responsibility to designate what equipment its employees may carry. This caselaw extends to both the guns and the ammo. This writer, while always hesitating to tell his subordinate officers what guns they could carry, has always specified what ammunition they may carry.

If your department has a wide open policy on the guns its personnel may carry, the only ammunition you should authorize for street carry carte blanche is the Remington jacketed hollowpoint. The entire line of Remington JHP ammo for police automatic calibers — .380, 9mm. Parabellum, .38 Super, and .45 ACP — was designed to be jacketed up and over the hollow cavity with tough copper, to prevent deforming in the feed ramp. The ogive (curve of the bullet shape) of each cartridge was designed to duplicate full metal jacket round-nose ammo. Result: any gun in the above calibers that feeds 100% with "hardball" ammo will almost certainly feed 100% with Remington hollowpoint.

The ogive shape and thoroughly jacketed hollow tip is at once the strength and the weakness of Remington ammo. The good news is that it always feeds, but the bad news is that it does not always expand in flesh and mushroom the way a hollowpoint anti-personnel bullet is intended to do. Sometimes it does, sometimes it doesn't.

Example: A New Jersey State Trooper shoots a suspect once with 115-grain Remington JHP out of his P7. The bullet strikes the heart, deforms, stays inside the body, and kills the suspect instantly.

Example: A lawman in Scottsdale, AZ, fires three rounds of the same Remington 115-gr. JHP into a suspect coming at him with a .22 automatic. All three strike, and the suspect instantly falls and dies. However, two of the three bullets pass completely through the suspect, showing limited deformation; had bystanders been behind this suspect, they might have been hit and crippled or killed.

Certain bullet designs work more effectively in the auto pistol. The Super Vel .45 and the similar hollowpoint load by Federal, 5 grains apart in bullet weight, both showed surprisingly good deformation in human flesh in actual police shootings. Really, it wasn't that surprising: both cartridge manufacturers bought their almost identical bullets from the same outside subcontractor. Both generally stayed in the felon's body and delivered tremendous stopping power.

However, that bullet did not feed in all factory-stock Colts and war surplus privately owned weapons that found their way into the police service. Thus, Federal changed their bullet design to one with a more tightly closed nose, which would now feed like the Remington, but like the Remington, wouldn't always be guaranteed to expand.

The Winchester Silvertip, designed to be the ultimate police hollow-point, did in fact beat everything else in tests in "flesh simulating media", but did not perform nearly that well in actual shootings. Like the Remington, the Silvertip sometimes mushroomed and sometimes didn't. In the one incident where Illinois State Police used first generation 9mm. Silvertip, the suspect had to be shot 13 times: 8 of the bullets went all the way through, and of the five that stayed in, only three really expanded, though at least two of the exiting bullets showed evidence of having been mushroomed by the time they left the body.

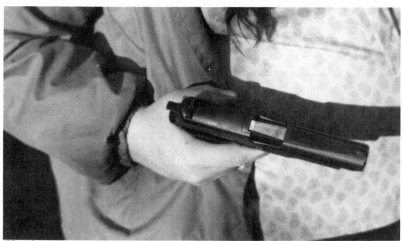

*When firing from the close combat or "protected gun" position, slide can foul with jacket or other clothing and jam gun unless this technique is used: gun is rotated 45° to outside so slide and spent casings can clear the body and clothing.*

A relatively rare problem has been *unintentional disassembly of the police service auto.* Badly worn Colts, and first or second generation Smith & Wesson automatics, were known to lock up or worse after the first one or two shots were fired if someone had applied pressure to the take-down stud, that is, the part of the slide stop that protrudes from the right side of the frame on such pistols. One would assume that this is the reason why third generation Smith & Wesson semiautomatic police pistols have that stud recessed into the frame, where only intentional pressure can begin disassembly.

The superbly functional P7 pistol by H&K has a problem in this regard: the takedown button on the frame is located directly under the grooves on the slide that are designed for the shooter's fingers to be manipulating. I am now up to five students using P7s who have been forced to rack the slide under great pressure and have inadvertently disassembled their pistols in the process.

The solution is simple, one the HK people should have thought of: grind down the takedown button flush with the frame, so that someone who intentionally wished to disassemble their pistol would have to use a punch, or the nose of a bullet, to do so. I am amazed that the HK Police Armorer's School does not mention this. They should.

Officers carrying the first two generations of 9mm. Smith autos, Browning Hi-Powers, or Colt 1911 pattern pistols can theoretically try to grind down the takedown studs on the slide stops but, in practice, can solve the problem simply by using the LFI technique for holding the trigger finger out of the trigger guard. It is a straight trigger finger outside the guard that causes this problem with such pistols, while it is overhand manipulation of the slide that causes it to occur with the P7.

There is a tendency for some auto pistols to *release their magazines prematurely.* I have found that this is likely to occur with any of the Smith & Wesson 9mm. pistols, occurs almost epidemically with the downscaled .380 caliber Colt Government pistol, and happens in the full-sized Colt Government and Commander and 1911 pistols only when the officer has modified his weapon with aftermarket oversized magazine release buttons and/or lightened magazine release springs.

Elsewhere in this book, we recount graphic real-life cases in which the magazine disconnector safety of the Smith & Wesson 9mm. autos kept disarmed officers from being killed. An overview of the collective real-world police experience with auto pistols equipped with magazine disconnector safeties shows that they have saved more lives than they have cost. In fairness, however, one should consider the officers who have been hurt because of the feature.

One northwestern police officer, shortly after the first generation S&W 9mm. got a reputation, started carrying one. Faced with a knife-armed suspect who was coming at him, he drew his m/39 and pulled the trigger, but the gun didn't go off. The long magazine release button on his early model pistol had contacted the inside edge of his holster hard enough to release the clip and activate the disconnector safety. The officer was badly cut up in this encounter. As a direct result of this incident, Smith & Wesson reduced the size of the model 39's magazine release button, and J.M. Bucheimer, manufacturer of the involved officer's holster, designed a new holster for the m/39 with a cutout where the mag release button was located, so it could no longer press against the release button hard enough to drop the mag and deactivate the gun.

Yet even this was not enough. After two midwestern officers were shot as a result of the failure of such a pistol to fire, multiple incidents came to light of cops who had been carrying S&W 9mm.s that couldn't fire because the mag release had been touched and the magazine disconnector safety thus rendered the weapon unshootable.

The case that brought this to light was Scott & Lampe v. Smith & Wesson. Scott and Lampe were two county police officers entering the den of a drug dealer, upon warrant. When the doper emerged from the shadows and levelled his autoloading rifle on Scott, Scott tried to bring up his S&W model 59 and shoot him. But as he went into his Weaver Stance, he inadvertently touched the mag release button on the pistol, dropping the clip and rendering the chambered round unshootable. Scott pulled the trigger with no effect, and the doper shot him in the chest.

As he fell, Scott tried to yell a warning to Lampe. He couldn't; he had a bullet through his lung. As Lampe entered the kill zone, the drug dealer opened up on him with the rifle, shooting him fatally through heart and spine.

Smith & Wesson settled out of court the morning of trial. The problem had not been the magazine disconnector safety, which had saved so many lives in other cases when perpetrators had grabbed guns from cops, or kids had gotten hold of their dads' pistols; the problem had been that, as an S&W engineer admitted in sworn deposition testimony, Smith & Wesson had copied the Colt magazine release devices slavishly in all respects except one. Thinking the 8-pound release on the Colt mag was too hard for a fast reload, they had cut the spring tension in half, to four pounds. It was THIS that led to all the accidental magazine releases on S&W 9mm. pistols, including the one that got Lampe killed and Scott shot, in my opinion.

This tells you something. Whatever S&W automatic you own, bring it to your department armorer or local certified S&W gunsmith, and have him lengthen the spring or install another to bring the magazine release up to eight pounds of resistance. I learned this lesson from one bullet-scarred cop, and from the widow of a dead one: Scott wouldn't have been wounded and Lampe wouldn't have been killed, in my opinion, if the S&W automatic in question had had an 8-pound mag release spring.

*First generation model 39 auto had numerous shortcomings. The only problem author feels remains in updated versions is light magazine release spring; retrofit with 8 lb. tension is suggested.*

To summarize, if you grind down the takedown button on your HK P7 and have an armorer or gunsmith install an 8-pound magazine release on your Smith & Wesson automatic, you won't have to worry about the gun falling apart while you're trying to shoot it.

If you have an auto pistol with a European style butt-catch magazine release, such as the German P9S, the Browning BDA in 9mm., .38 Super, or .45, or the identical SIG-Sauer P-220 of pre-1986/7 vintage, or an early P7, you don't want to be firing the gun from a fast prone position or bracing its butt on a hard horizontal cover surface. This is because recoil can drive the butt hard enough against the ground (indeed, thrusting the gun forward against the ground in prone position can do it) to release the magazine and inadvertently unload your pistol. At the prestigious Bianchi Cup, top contenders Jerry Usher and Nick Pruitt did just that to their P9S autos when they went prone. It cost them each the most famous and prestigious handgun match in the world. . . but on the street, it could have cost them their lives, as they were both acutely aware. Usher shot his next Bianchi Cup with a Smith & Wesson revolver, Pruitt with a side-release Colt .45 automatic.

**The bottom line is this: Some automatics jam more often than revolvers, but good, carefully selected automatics do not. Some cartridges will jam automatics, but there are many good jacketed hollow-point police loads that will not.**

*Auto pistol malfunctions must be kept in perspective: revolvers jam, too. This Smith & Wesson model 65 service revolver is solidly jammed with .38 Special shell casing trapped under the ejector star, will take far longer to clear than most auto pistol stoppages.*

**Auto pistols may jam when fired from alongside barricade cover, but they won't if you use the proper techniques. Some automatics can accidentally dump their magazines or fall apart or go off if dropped or if someone struggles for them, but you can solve that by either authorizing different automatics or compensating for the problem in training, or by having your armorer make minor but important corrections to the issue guns.**

*(Left) To unload, one first places safety "on" if design allows; note safety on position of slide-mounted safety catch on this S&W 669 demonstrated by Police Chief Cameron Harbison, a southpaw. Then, magazine is withdrawn from the butt. (Center) Removed magazine is now put away (pocket or waistband, or as author prefers, tucked under gun arm). This forces arm to lock against body, naturally locking the gun in the safe downrange position. Magazine should NOT be placed in firing hand, which weakens grasp on still-live pistol and can dangerously complicate unloading of chamber. (Right) With gun hand still holding pistol, slide is pulled sharply to rear by weak hand. Chambered round ejects (seen here falling past knee of Chief Harbison) and drops to the ground. Pistol is then laid down or holstered, and dropped cartridge retrieved. On some pistols, placing hand over ejection port and ejecting round into hand can cause cartridge blowup with severe hand damage if cartridge primer encounters ejector.*

*(Left) Safe loading and holstering. Slide of empty pistol is locked to the rear, and full magazine is inserted into the butt. When design allows, as on this S&W 669 9mm., safety catch should be in the "on" position. (Center) As magazine is slapped firmly home, slide is dropped forward at full speed of spring (not "eased" forward as it would be with empty pistol). Officer at this point should check by sight and feel that magazine is fully inserted and cartridge has in fact been chambered. (Right) Holster weapon with index finger extended forward (to keep from catching it between edge of holster and trigger, causing accidental discharge) and use thumb to hold hammer in appropriate position, again to failsafe against accidental discharge. Safety strap is now fastened. If an additional cartridge must be inserted into the magazine, the magazine can be removed while pistol is in holster, extra round added, and magazine firmly reseated in holstered pistol.*

# SELECTION OF DEFENSIVE AUTOLOADER AMMO

Four criteria are vital to the selection of law enforcement ammunition: 1) Stopping Power, 2) Controllability, 3) Reduced Ricochet, and 4) Optimum Penetration.

*Stopping Power* is critical since the only time the officer is justified in firing his gun at a perpetrator is when the latter is doing something so dangerous to innocent human life that he must be stopped *immediately,* indeed, stopped so decisively that he cannot flick his trigger finger. In small and medium caliber handguns, this requires expanding bullets; even in larger calibers, expanding bullets magnify stopping power. The collective military and police experience *with fully jacketed "hardball" pistol ammo* shows that only the .45 caliber, by virtue of its weight, mass, and cross-section, seems to strike hard enough to reliably stop a fight more than half the time with a single torso hit. Independent studies by Sgt. Evan Marshall and this writer indicate approximately 68% and 70% stopping power capability with one round of .45 hardball; both found the better 9mm. hollowpoints to have virtually identical stopping power. These figures came from documented street shootings of armed human beings, not from laboratory experiments in "test media". Such tests often erroneously show 9mm. hollowpoint and even 9mm. hardball to have dramatically more stopping power than .45 ball. This is diametrically opposed to street and battlefield observations with both cartridges since before WWI.

*Not all police loads work as well in flesh as in gelatin. Federal Nyclad 9mm. worked great in test media as shown here, but Federal officials privately admitted disappointing performance in the field. Photo courtesy Federal Cartridge.*

*Controllability* is vital since officers are more likely now than ever to have to fire multiple times in a confrontation. This is due to three factors: a) increasing potential of facing a drilled team of multiple criminal opponents; b) proliferation of crack, PCP, and other drugs that allow the user to absorb an enormous amount of punishment and continue homicidal assault; and c) increased use of soft body armor by criminals.

"Controllability" means the ability of the officer to recover from the recoil of one shot sufficiently to accurately fire the following shot, no matter what scenario has forced him to fire multiple times. There are many factors here: the weight and design of the weapon, the axis of the bore, the design of the pistol's internal operation, and perhaps most important, the training of the officer.

A pistol with a higher bore axis, like the SIG P-220, will flip its muzzle slightly higher than an equal weight, but lower bore axis, Colt LW Commander if both are fired from the same hand and same stance with the same .45 load. The HK P7's gas operation system bleeds off some of the recoil force and is one reason most users perceive this full-power 9mm. Parabellum handgun to recoil more like the .380 (9mm. Short) caliber, a much less powerful weapon. The all-stainless-steel S&W model 639 is generally perceived as "kicking" markedly less than the aluminum framed model 439, which is identical except for being lighter.

Most important, however, is the training of the officer. Properly trained with a StressFire Isosceles or a Weaver Stance, the officer with the hardest kicking .45 will show more controllability in accurate, rapid fire than the officer in a poor, off-balance stance even if the latter is armed with the lightest-recoil .380.

*It is widely believed that Weaver stance is best for autos, Isosceles better for service revolvers. In fact, either technique works with either gun. Choice is dependent on physiology of the shooter.*

*After these auto shooters were familiarized with both Weaver and Isosceles techniques, they were encouraged to use whichever method worked better for them. Class is LFI-II.*

*LFI staffer Rick Devoid adjusts this student into a perfect StressFire Isosceles position. Body weight is totally forward behind gun, torso is squared to target to maximize vest protection in real-life firefight. Student in background is applying similar principles with Weaver stance.*

*In one-handed shooting training, remember that grip and arm must be rigid (StressFire Shotokan Punch technique is shown here). If wrist is limp, part of slide's momentum dissipates through frame during recoil and slide doesn't go all the way back, causing pistol to jam.*

Controllability is a factor that will vary between individuals, weapons, cartridges, and training systems. With proper training, any 9mm., .38 Super, or .45 autoloader can be learned by *any* non-handicapped adult male or female, no matter what their size. This is *not* necessarily true of certain police revolver calibers, such as .357 Magnum and .41 Magnum.

*Author supervises a mixed revolver/auto class in Los Angeles. Cliff Stewart, whose .45 auto has just locked slide back after last shot, is Mr. T's bodyguard.*

*Reduced Ricochet* is critical since, in a real-world encounter, the officer may well be firing on an angle and under circumstances where his bullet could strike a hard surface and glance off at an unpredictable angle, creating danger of death or grave bodily harm to innocent bystanders. This situation is enhanced in urban areas, where the hard and geometrically straight surfaces of "the concrete canyon" become "ricochet city".

Round nose, full metal jacket bullets are extremely prone to ricochet. Jacketed hollowpoints with very steep ogives (i.e., angles of shape similar to round nose) also present a significant ricochet problem.

*Optimum Penetration* is perhaps the most difficult factor to determine and provide for. The officer wants a bullet that will go through medium-density cover an opponent might hide behind, such as furniture or car doors, yet will not rip completely through a house. It is particularly important that the bullet stay inside the human body without exiting. This is because: (a) a bullet that stays in dumps all its energy for maximum shock power, while the bullet that exits merely "bumps the suspect on the way through"; and (b) the bullet that exits will endanger innocent persons located behind the perpetrator. Due to tunnel vision or simply the physical bulk of the criminal suspect blocking the officer's view, this becomes a very real hazard.

Some rounds that have reputations for good stopping power are disallowed in any real-world study of the penetration factor. For instance, .45 hardball has very good stopping power, yet such a bullet fired at close range from a 5 " barrel service automatic is statistically likely to completely exit the human body with more than enough power to kill an innocent person on the other side. .45 hardball is also notorious for ricochet.

It has long been recognized in police circles that hollowpoint bullets are the least likely to ricochet *or* to exit the suspect. While any bullet can ricochet if it strikes a hard surface at a sufficiently acute angle, and no bullet can be expected to stay in the body if it hits on the periphery or in such a way that it meets no heavy bone and muscle resistance, civil liability and simple morality indicate that the chosen round be the cartridge that ricochets least and overpenetrates least while still fulfilling the other criteria.

Stopping power, controllability, reduced ricochet, and optimum penetration are the basic four requirements of *any* police/self-defense cartridge. With the semiautomatic pistol, a fifth criterion must be added: *Reliability.*

The feed cycle mechanism of the semiautomatic pistol requires car-

*Extreme rapid fire should be only a relatively small part of the training course, so as not to encourage "spray and pray" tactics that could endanger bystanders on street. These LFI-2 shooters in Indiana work on burst fire; note "fountain of brass" from semiauto Glock-17 in foreground.*

tridges of certain *shape, pressure, and recoil impulse* if the mechanism is to feed the cartridge, fire it, and self-cycle at the proper speed and rate. While the revolver can be loaded with high or low velocity, high or low recoil, flat point or cup point or round nose bullets, the autoloader is much more demanding.

*Study of police gun battles shows that officers almost always lose count of rounds after first few shots are fired, and in a high-volume firefight will run gun completely dry. Accordingly, at least half of reloading training should require officers to recharge guns that have been run all the way to slidelock. LFI-2 class shown is in New Hampshire.*

Exposed soft lead at the bullet tip can strike the feed ramp and deform, jamming the pistol. A low-powered round will not generate enough recoil to operate the slide and cycle the automatic feed mechanism. A too-high-powered round may cycle the slide too rapidly to pick up the next cartridge at the appropriate point. A very light, high-velocity round may have a pressure curve that peaks too soon, and when fired in a pistol whose slide mass and spring compression rate are designed for standard rounds, may cause the slide to start back suddenly, then run out of inertia and fail to complete its cyclic movement. A cartridge that is too short overall or too wide and sharp-edged in the bullet nose area may hit the feed ramp at the wrong angle and jam the weapon.

Several years ago, a study by a gunwriter trying to determine the ideal police handgun settled on the not-yet-perfected Smith & Wesson model 59, despite the fact that his own tests rated it as mediocre for functioning with police ammunition. He felt that in such areas as compactness and firepower the 59 is/was so superior to other police handguns existing at the time as to overwhelm the feeding problems on total points. The gunwriter was not, obviously, a policeman, or the model 59 would have been thrown out at the beginning of his tests. No matter what other attributes it has, an item of safety-rescue equipment must prove itself utterly reliable *before other points are even considered.* The police/self-defense side arm is just that, an item of emergency rescue equipment that will be employed "for real" only when human lives are in the balance. In that context, reliability is where we start from in the evaluation of equipment. Accuracy, appearance, and versatility are negotiable. Reliability is not.

This is why, for so many years, departments issuing 9mm. and .45 automatics permitted only hardball ammo. Aware that stopping power was being compromised along with safety from ricochet and overpenetration, departments accepted that balance of risk to guarantee that the weapon would work and fire every time. That was because high-performance ammunition at that time could not meet the first four criteria and still perform reliably.

Fortunately, this is no longer the case. Both the firearms industry and the ammo makers have offered solutions which, taken together, make *reliable* jacketed hollowpoint ammo that meets the four criteria, available for all police calibers.

At this writing, the rounds that have the best track records based on independent monitoring of police shootings around the country are the following:

*.380 ACP: The Winchester Silvertip.* This round has an extremely con-

sistent rate of expansion and almost never exits the body with a solid hit, despite the low velocity. This does not mean that every perpetrator shot with it drops like a rock. The Silvertip allows the .380 to spend all its energy inside the hostile target, but being a low-powered round, it doesn't have that much energy to spend. Fortunately, the .380 is accepted to be a last-ditch weapon used by undercover people who need to appear unarmed, by off-duty officers in the lowest possible threat scenarios, and by officers who are acutely conscious of size and bulk in a backup weapon and, absent the small, flat .380 auto, might carry no backup at all.

The *only* factory-produced gun that will, out of the box, feed this cartridge has been the SIG-Sauer P-230, in my experience. Walthers generally need to have the feed ramp and chamber mouth "throated" for this or any other effective hollowpoint.

*9mm. Parabellum:* The three most commonly used police rounds in this weapon are the 115-grain jacketed hollowpoints produced by Remington, Federal, and Winchester. Increasing in popularity is the BAT round, which will be discussed separately under "Exotic Ammunition".

The Remington was the first hollowpoint that would reliably feed in first and second generation defensive 9mm.s (S&W model 39, etc.). This was because, like all of the Remington line of jacketed hollowpoint auto pistol ammo, the bullet was designed to duplicate hardball in shape, with a copper jacket coming up and over the edges of the hollow cavity so no exposed lead could deform and jam on the feed ramp. Unfortunately, this also made expansion less likely, thus compromising three of the basic criteria (stopping power, optimum penetration, and reduced ricochet). While the New Jersey State Police has had very good luck with this load, we also have numerous cases on record where the bullet failed to expand and went all the way through the suspect, requiring follow-up shots and potentially endangering bystanders. Still, the Remington hollowpoint is far less offensive in these respects than any conventional 9mm. hardball load, has much more stopping power, and is the only factory hollowpoint at this time likely to feed in such popular, factory-stock pistols as the conventional Browning P-35 Hi-Power, or the many older-model S&W 9mm.s still in service.

Winchester's Silvertip has gone through many drastic modifications since it was first introduced in the late 1970s. All original tests were based on flesh-simulating media (Duxseal, etc.), and Winchester found themselves making a round that worked great on duct sealant and somewhat less spectacularly on living tissue. The aluminum jacket of the original Silvertip also required a special lubricant, which unfortunately would melt at about 140° Fahrenheit. The melted lube would ooze down into the gunpowder, contaminating it and creating a dud round. There were also numerous reports of the aluminum jacket flaking or even peeling off inside the barrels. Some of these problems were solved with a subsequent generation of Silvertip, which had a copper jacket that was nickel-plated to preserve the distinctive Silvertip look, but a main problem remained: the bullet often went all the way through a suspect, failing to open and delivering poor shock effect.

By early 1986, police departments had access to third generation Silvertip, which combined the improved jacket-and-lube compositions with a very deeply serrated jacket, reminiscent of the 112-grain Super Vel 9mm. hollowpoint introduced in the early '80s. Almost saw-toothed at the tip of the hollow cavity, this round did seem to peel back its jacket and mushroom effectively. Las Vegas Metro PD, which went to this design after several stopping failures with its previous soft-nose 9mm. issue load, had ten consecutive 9mm. shootings in which they deemed the new-generation Silvertip to have performed superbly. Says Undersheriff Eric Cooper of LVMPD, "This round restored our men's faith in the 9mm. as a service weapon they could rely on."

In San Diego, where 9mm. autos had been a "limited option" weapon for certain officers, earlier Silvertip had performed poorly. Lt. John Morrison of San Diego PD recalls one case in which a missed projectile went through considerable depths of furniture and walls, only by circumstance not hitting an innocent, while the suspect took two more unexpanded bullets that went through and through him with poor stopping effect. A switch to the latest generation Silvertip, said Morrison, turned that around: every subsequent shooting resulted in good stops, good expansions, and optimum penetration.

Through this entire period, however, a less heavily advertised police cartridge was building a much more enviable reputation: Federal's "9BP" load. The 9 BP appeared to be an ordinary jacketed hollowpoint, but its performance was phenomenal. The chief medical examiner of a large California county told world pistol champ Ray Chapman that this bullet caused more destruction in human flesh than any other handgun round he'd seen, including .357 Magnum, and he had seen a lot of it since the 9 BP was issue for a major department in his county that was involved in numerous shootings. In separate tests conducted for GUN WORLD'S publishing group by authorities Dean Grennell, Wiley Clapp, and Claud Hamilton, all came separately to the conclusion that the 9 BP was by far the most accurate round in every 9mm. Parabellum service pistol *and* target pistol tested.

This writer had come separately to the same conclusion. Tom Campbell of Smith & Wesson, who for many years was considered the world's most formidable competitor with a 9mm. pistol, made a point of shooting only the Federal 9 BP round after *his* independent tests confirmed it to be by far the most accurate. This writer, after testing and also inputting Campbell's information, also used this round every time he shot a 9mm. competition; two of his three national records were set with this cartridge, fired from the HK P9S Sport Target 9mm. Sgt. Gary Paul Johnston of Shaker Heights, OH, PD, one of the country's most knowledgeable shooters and police weapons experts, reports that his department settled on this cartridge for their issue S&W 9mm. service pistols.

Of the three major brands, this Federal 9mm. JHP has had by far the least failures according to the writer's research. When an article to this effect was published nationally in a combat handgun magazine, two complaints came in: one alleged that Las Vegas Metro had experienced numerous stopping failures with the Federal 9mm. hollowpoint, and another alleged that Ft. Lauderdale, FL, PD had gone through the same problem. Follow-up by this writer showed that Vegas Metro had issued Federal 95-grain soft-nose 1,200 fps velocity ammo, not the 115-grain hollowpoint at the same velocity, during the time the problems were experienced, and had never issued the 9 BP. A Ft. Lauderdale PD spokesman advised that he could only document two shootings in which the 9 BP had "failed". In one, the suspect was shot through the muscle of the thigh, with the bullet never touching bone or a major blood vessel; the suspect then surrendered and walked to the patrol car. In another case, the suspect was shot through the chest with the bullet entering below the shoulder blade and passing between the posterior ribs, coursing through the lung and exiting between two anterior ribs through the chest. The spokesman stated that the exit hole was "about the size of a nickel", and that immediately after being shot this suspect ceased hostile action and ran from the scene, dropping dead from loss of blood some 200 yards away.

*No* bullet through the thigh that does not damage the femoral artery, the femur, or the common peroneal nerve can be expected to put a man down, and even if all three have been destroyed the suspect can simply rock his weight onto the other leg and stay upright for 90 seconds or more, still fighting, even if the femoral artery is bleeding freely. The thigh is simply not a "stopping zone".

Similarly, a pure "lung shot" is, in the parlance of medical examiners, "an adynamic hit", meaning that it does not usually cause death or immediate or significant incapacitation. It was against the odds, but by no means unusual for this bullet to have exited after going through intercostal spaces (between the ribs) on both sides of the body. Had the bullet struck bone, the likelihood of it staying inside and doing major damage would have been enhanced. Yet, the bullet was obviously fully mushroomed to have created the size exit hole it did, and the nature of the damage from a usually adynamic hit was enough to cause the suspect to bleed out and die after running 200 yards. Given the fact that the average man can run 200 yards in around 30 seconds, and considering the other aspects of the two shootings, this writer does not believe either of the Ft. Lauderdale incidents is a "stopping failure" of the 9 BP Federal load.

In the early and mid-eighties, the 9 BP was modified with serrated jacket and a wider hollowpoint. Excellent performance continues.

The 9 BP Federal, like the Winchester Silvertip, will feed with total reliability in third generation S&Ws, HK P7s, and Beretta and SIG-Sauer 9mm.s. Based on research, the author's first choice is the 9 BP, second choice the latest Silvertip, in conventional U.S.-made ammo for police 9mm. Parabellum pistols. In older style guns (Colt, Browning) that have not been custom "throated", Remington 115-grain JHP is the load of choice.

*So few shootings occur with police-type loadings in .38 Super that author cannot recommend a reliably performing cartridge for the caliber. This Remington +P 115-grain hollowpoint seems promising, but with so many other calibers having established track records in police shootings, "promising" doesn't count.*

*.38 Super.* Though gun experts consider the .38 Super to be potentially the ideal police cartridge, no major department has adopted this load for service. The gunfight statistics available for it are almost entirely built around the load that has been standard for this weapon since its inception circa 1930: a 130-grain "hardball" bullet at somewhat over 1,200 feet per second velocity. The Super usually delivers stopping power in this configuration only if it hits heavy bone.

Due to a semi-rimmed design, it long had a well-deserved reputation for poor accuracy. The SIG-Sauer P-220 and the retrofit Bar-Sto barrel for Colts in this caliber both headspace on the case mouth, greatly improving accuracy. The Astra A-80, the only high-capacity version of the .38 Super now in use, does not have sufficient representation in law enforcement to have developed a track record one way or the other.

Rounds available include the Winchester Silvertip and Remington hollowpoint, both of which are essentially higher-velocity versions of the same cartridges in 9mm. While they theoretically should perform better in .38 Super than in 9mm. Parabellum, no actual street gunfight data exists due to the unpopularity of the round, which has kept it out of the "gunfight data base". In law enforcement at this time, the .38 Super is usually encountered only as the personally-owned weapon of a police gun buff who is seeking maximum performance.

Another problem with the .38 Super is that in conventional loadings, it is rated to penetrate most police body armor now in use. Remember, the cartridge was designed in 1930 to allow lawmen to shoot through fleeing Ford V-8 automobiles. Despite its great promise with hollowpoints, the .38 Super has not yet had a chance, in any cartridge conformation, to prove itself as a law enforcement weapon.

*.45 ACP.* The .45 ACP (Automatic Colt Pistol) was the first auto pistol cartridge to find favor with police. From the beginning, such gun-savvy departments as the Texas Rangers carried it as an optional weapon. A considerable data base exists on performance of various rounds in this gun, since like any military weapon it has become popular among the public, who use it sometimes with cartridges other than GI ball. Still, 230-grain hardball is by far the most commonly encountered .45 ACP cartridge used in actual shootings in the United States, even by police.

The first effective jacketed hollowpoint factory load for the .45 auto was the Super Vel, and because a high percentage of those officers carrying .45s were knowledgeable about guns and sought out the best ammo (and because many such officers were in high-risk assignments like Stakeout and Narcotics), a data base became established with unusual speed. In most cases, the Super Vel bullet expanded very well and stopped gunfights with one hit well over three-fourths of the time, a better record than hardball. It usually also stayed in the body.

Remington was the first "major" manufacturer to come out with a .45 hollowpoint. This 185-grain load was jacketed up and over the hollow cavity, yet in the first few shootings after its introduction in the early '70s, developed an excellent reputation for opening up and giving top stopping power. This reputation waned slightly as Remington apparently toughened the jacket, reducing the bullet's ability to expand. Our updated research shows that the bullet will exit about 30% of the time (compared to about 70% of the time with hardball), and because of the shape and the design of the jacket, it shares hardball's tendency to ricochet. However, since it feeds in virtually any .45 that feeds ball (including the old, military surplus, and off-brand .45s accepted by many departments with privately owned, department-approved weapons policies), it is still a distinctly better performer than hardball and the best choice as an issue or authorized .45 round for departments that permit a broad range of .45 caliber pistols.

*Remington 185-grain hollowpoint feeds in any old-generation .45 auto that feeds hardball. This is Springfield Armory's well-made but military-spec 1911-A1 service pistol.*

The Federal 185-grain bullet duplicated the ballistics of the Remington cartridge at about 935 feet per second velocity from a 5″ barrel service pistol (compared to GI hardball's 230-grain slug at 830 fps). However, a wider mouth and softer lead made it almost guaranteed to expand. Independent tests done at LFI showed that this was the least likely round to go through multiple walls, etc., when fired in a dwelling, and also noted enormous expansion and dramatic shock effect in living tissue. Unfortunately, the wide mouth required a throated pistol for feeding reliability; and to satisfy a public that was often buying ammo for old fashioned military surplus guns, Federal in first quarter 1986 redesigned the bullet with a smaller, more jacketed-over nose. This equalled the Remington for feeding reliability, but also caused the bullet to mushroom slightly less and penetrate slightly more.

*Cartridges for modern police service use should be jacketed hollowpoints to reduce ricochet and overpenetration that would otherwise endanger innocents and brother officers, and to amplify stopping power without increasing lethality. Shown is a Federal 185-grain .45 hollowpoint cartridge, and a bullet from same recovered from pig killed by author with this 5" barrel Colt service automatic. Note excellent mushrooming in living flesh and bone.*

Winchester's Silvertip .45, like the 9mm., was not at first the cartridge it promised to be. There were numerous cases of it penetrating far too deeply, often without significant expansion. In a Denver area case, a very large and heavy man was shot widthways through the middle of the torso with a Silvertip out of a 4¼" barrel Colt Commander .45. The bullet destroyed his heart and dropped him instantly, but barely kept from exiting; autopsy photos show it protruding from the exit wound, its hollow nose completely undeformed. Had the suspect been smaller or had the shot been front to back, the bullet almost certainly would have gone through him and struck one of the other officers who were in a ring-formation around the knife-armed suspect at the time of the shooting.

In a northern Illinois shooting that was touted as a success for the Silvertip, investigation of the actual circumstances leaves room for argument. The armed would-be cop-killer was shot four times in rapid succession by Silvertips from police .45 automatics. One bullet entered the side of the head just below the ear, and went completely through and through despite penetration of massive maxillo-facial bone. As the suspect bent forward, two more bullets caught him between neck and shoulder on either side, ranging down; both stayed in the body with unimpressive expansion, but stopped only when they reached the intestines. They had literally gone through two feet or more of human flesh before stopping. A fourth round did, however, expand well and stay in the body as designed. These, according to the investigator, were first generation Silvertips with aluminum jackets and no jacket serrations.

As with third generation 9mm. Silvertips, the latest Silvertip .45 ACPs seem to be performing somewhat better, but since the .45 is now far less common in U.S. police circles than the 9mm., there is not nearly as large a data base from police shootings.

A fourth U.S.-made jacketed hollowpoint load for the .45 ACP is of significant interest. This is the CCI-Speer 200-grain "Inspector", a part of the "Lawman" series of ammunition from that company. This cartridge has existed unchanged for several years and is unique in that, while it is generally too expensive to be adopted by departments on bid, it is so popular among the gun-wise officers on optional-weapon departments that a workable data base has nonetheless been established.

The Speer load has been dubbed "the flying ashtray", since its hollow cavity is so wide it can literally swallow a .32 slug. It is also a short bullet in a short cartridge, and the combination of wide and short dimensions create significant feeding problems in most older, military style .45 autoloaders. Most factory Colts won't feed this round reliably, and many early-generation SIG P-220s will occasionally jam with it. However, the Smith & Wesson 645 police service auto seems to feed it 100%, as do recent production runs of the P-220. Colt automatics, modified by Bill Laughridge of Cylinder & Slide Shop, Fremont, Nebraska, were found to feed this cartridge reliably in more than twenty tested specimens.

While the top-quality Speer brass-case load is significantly more expensive than hollowpoints produced by Remington and Federal, an identical-length cartridge with aluminum case and the same bullet is produced in Speer's line of economical "Blazer" disposable-case ammunition. This makes the Speer actually a best-buy item, when considering the amount of duty-type practice ammo that must be consumed to establish reliability of the gun and documentable competency of the shooter.

The Speer 200-grain .45 load is unquestionably the most powerful conventional round available in this caliber. The 200-grain bullet leaves the muzzle at an honest 1,000 feet per second, creating significantly more energy and impact than either the standard 185-grain/935 fps hollowpoints by Winchester, Federal, and Remington, *or* the ubiquitous 230-grain/830 fps hardball load. Simply shooting reaction targets with all three ammo types will show that the momentum of the Speer load flattens a steel disk more rapidly than any of the others.

Shooting reports indicate that, like the other three brands of hollowpoint, the Speer will *probably* expand when fired from a 5″ barrel, may or may not when fired from a 4¼″ barrel, and probably *won't* expand when fired from a compact, 3½″ barrel .45 automatic. However, in the great majority of cases, *the bullet will stay in the body whether it expands or not, and will dump all its energy there.* A shooting in the Chicago area became famous when multiple gunwriters heard about it and reported that the three Speer hollowpoints fired into the deceased had failed to expand; this was cited as an argument for staying with hardball. However, investigation shows that all three bullets stayed in the body, and the subject struck by the rapid fire burst instantly fell dead. The shots were fired from a stubby-barrelled Detonics .45 autoloader.

*Note excellent expansion of this CCI Speer Inspector load, a 200-grain jacketed hollowpoint used by author to kill a hog instantly with one shot from 4¼″ barrel Colt Commander .45 ACP.*

*As an administrative lieutenant in charge of training, author's present duty weapon is this lightweight Colt Commander .45 tuned for "court resistant duty use" by Bill Laughridge of Cylinder & Slide Shop, Fremont, NE. Duty load is CCI Speer Lawman 200-gr. JHP. Practice load is inexpensive, disposable case Blazer by same firm with same bullet. An important police auto advantage is that only full power loads will operate the gun, hence all practice fire is "job related" with equivalent flash, blast, and recoil for civil liability reasons as well as practicality.*

The writer has only one shooting report of this bullet exiting a suspect, a Texas gunman who was shot side-to-side (through soft abdominal tissue) by a cop with a .45. Even though the bullet exited, the suspect instantly collapsed and died on the spot with no further hostilities.

More typical are cases like my student who shot a suspect in the knee with this bullet at some 25 yards from a Colt Gold Cup. The suspect dropped at the moment of the shot, rendered unconscious by shock. The bullet fragmented and did not exit; and while doctors were able to save the limb, it is now vestigial and several inches shorter than its mate.

One of my clients shot a suspect at a range of a few inches, just below the mouth with the same bullet, also out of a Gold Cup and travelling 1,000 fps. The detailed medical report clearly indicates "total avulsion of the lower mandible", that is, the lower jaw was completely blown away from the face from the canine teeth forward. The bullet fragmented and joined the spray of bloody mist and bone particles that spewed from the side-to-side shot. The suspect, incidentally, survived, though his seven-figure lawsuit against the officer did not.

J. Michael Plaxco, the noted combat pistol champion, was at first disappointed in this round when he shot a deer with it from a range of 50 yards and it ran about the same distance before dropping dead. The bullet did not expand. Analysis shows that a .45 ACP slug always loses velocity very rapidly as distance increases, and the bullet that struck the deer at 50 yards would have been travelling at the same speed as a close-range shot from a 3.5 " barrel instead of Plaxco's 5 ". The bullet stayed inside the animal, expending all its energy even though it didn't expand. Plaxco later came to realize that, all things considered, the bullet had done its job and stopped the deer with a chest hit about as well as a hit in the same place with a high-powered .30/06 hunting rifle. (Indeed, legendary handgun hunter Hal Swiggett has shot many deer-size animals with the Remington 185-grain hollowpoint fired from his 5 " Colt .45 automatic and reports that it drops deer, a man-size mammal, faster than most high-powered rifles in his considerable experience.)

## Soft-Nose Ammunition

The collective law enforcement experience with soft-nose police auto pistol ammo indicates that it is a poor substitute for jacketed hollow-points. The only soft-nose auto pistol bullet that ever fulfilled the four criteria was Federal's special Illinois State Police load, a dish-nosed 95-grain Hornady bullet loaded at high pressure to an honest 1,400 feet per second out of a 4 " barrel. While it did not shoot through cars, it was proven in its several ISP shootouts to almost always stay in the body with a good bullet placement and to deliver dramatic shock effect. When ISP dropped the load — because its short overall length did not allow 100 % feeding in second generation S&W pistols then issued — Federal kept the round in production. However, fearing that the high-powered load could blow up poor-quality pistols, Federal reduced the pressure and lowered velocity to 1,200 feet per second. Now exerting considerably less energy than a 115-grain hollowpoint bullet at the same velocity, even without consideration of the expansion factor, the once-excellent cartridge had "feebed out". The 1,200 fps version of the 9mm. softnose was the bullet that had performed so poorly in the Las Vegas Metro shootouts that officers demanded alternative weapons. A 1,300 fps Federal 95-grain JSP sold to LAPD did well in the first 14 shootings that agency recorded with 9mm.

Early writings on the 9mm. for self defense and police service use touted the Winchester PowerPoint 100-grain soft nose. Illinois State Police had this round for several years as issue, and the agency's gunfight statistics show two glaring flaws with it: every round fired into a felon's body completely exited, including shots into the thickest and heaviest parts of the body and skull, and the only instant one-shot stops that ever occurred with it involved central nervous system hits or, in one case, a contact distance shot to the right side that exploded the liver of the homicidal suspect with the "gas effect" of the muzzle blast.

At this time, absent loadings such as the special 95-grain Federal load now sold only on special contract to major police departments, *only* jacketed hollowpoints or certain exotic loads should be considered for the 9mm. No conventional soft point will do the police self-defense handgun's job reliably.

## ACLU/Geneva Convention Considerations

In the first half of the '70s, the American Civil Liberties Union mounted an effort to ban police use of hollowpoint ammunition. The continuing debates seemed, on the CLU side, to be taken word for word from an article in THE NATION magazine titled *"The Vietnamization of Main Street"*. We who fought for police use of appropriate equipment would hear again and again phrases like "Bullets shaped like the nacelles of jet engines" and "The bullet doesn't explode — *you* do!"

All this was easy to defeat with an honest, nonpartisan audience. You simply *showed* them the bullets that were being talked about, both unfired and fully mushroomed. You explained that the Geneva Conventions and the Hague Accords specifically exempted domestic problems from their covenants. You mentioned that if one went with the Geneva Convention, one could also inter prisoners for the "duration of the war on crime, until someone authorized to speak for them unilaterally surrendered", and until then could hold your criminals in POW camps. Theoretically, one could also nuke the Hell's Angels, napalm the bookie joints, and summarily execute any "out of uniform spy" who tried to assassinate a policeman. As Jeff Cooper suggested, "If they let the cops do everything else by the rules of war, I'm sure the cops will be thrilled to carry Geneva Convention bullets."

I found during those debates that other points came across well. The ACLU people were stunned to find out I was right when I told them that the 158-grain round-nose lead bullet they were urging cops to keep *also* violated the Geneva Convention and Hague Accords, which specifically forbade non-jacketed ammo, and no one on their side told them (until we humiliated them with it) that the full-jacketed bullets of the Rules of International Warfare are almost by definition armor-piercing projectiles that will ricochet madly down sidewalks and go through all manner of walls and criminal bodies to seek out more bystanders.

In the early 1970s, the New Hampshire Civil Liberties Union was chosen for the pilot project in which ACLU hoped to pass legislation to ban police use of hollowpoint bullets. The Massachusetts Civil Liberties Union had a bill in the hopper that would closely follow. I debated the leading proponent of that New Hampshire bill, Dudley Dudley, first in the pages of the liberal statewide weekly *New Hampshire Times*, and a second time on the floor of the New Hampshire State Senate. The *Times* debate clearly favored the police side — and the avowed liberal editor Richard Wright said at its conclusion, "Dudley, they've got you" — and the State Senate debate was particularly interesting.

Dudley had seen the writing on the wall and filibustered through almost the entire debate period allotted, leaving only twenty minutes for opposing comments. Earl Sweeney, then president of the New Hampshire Police Chiefs Association and at this writing director of the New Hampshire Police Standards and Training Council, stood up and said, "I implore you, ladies and gentlemen, to hear at least one person from our side, one nationally recognized expert." A crusty old Yankee on the Senate Judiciary Committee that was hearing the proposal said loudly, "I'd like to hear *something* expert about this." The Committee agreed, and I stepped forward to speak for the Chiefs' Association.

Twenty minutes wasn't a lot, but it was all that was necessary. The standard arguments went quick and fast — reduced likelihood of exit, reduced penetration, more stopping power — and then I dropped the bombshell: "Those who argue against hollowpoints don't understand the dynamics of gunfighting. If a Geneva Convention bullet goes through and through a man, not only does it go on, homing in on a baby carriage somewhere, but it only bumps him instead of slamming into him and stopping him. Now he has to be shot again and again.

"Such bullets create deeper wounds, obviously, and violate more bone structures, more organs, more blood vessels. They create another hole where air can rush in, creating pneumothorax and hemothorax, and promoting more hemorrhage. They are less survivable than hollowpoints!

"Any surgeon will confirm what I'm going to say," I continued. "The reason police went away from conventional bullets was that they went all the way through the body and didn't deliver stopping power, and the person had to be shot again and again. Ask any doctor: if the guy is shot six times, with at least four of the bullets going all the way through, there are six random wound tracks through vital organs and perhaps ten holes with air rushing in and blood rushing out. Compare that to one or two hollowpoints: the guy goes down, there is only one hole per shot to be sealed by the first responding rescuers; and there is a very high likelihood of survival if he is rushed to a good hospital. But shot several times with conventional bullets, even if the shooting goes down in the trauma ward of Mount Sinai Hospital during the surgeon's convention, there's a very small chance that the person will survive.

"Therefore, the police hollowpoint bullet is more humane for the person who has to be shot, as well as for the person who has to shoot him."

Throughout this hasty speech, I had noticed that the members of the Judiciary Committee kept throwing sidelong glances at a grey, wizened old Yankee at the middle of the table, who throughout was gently nodding in the affirmative. He turned out to be the one physician on the Committee. That body voted the bill to ban hollowpoints for police — which, by the way, expressly admitted that it could not ban them to anybody else! —"inexpedient to legislate."

The bill was dead. Massachusetts was the next step, and the Massachusetts Police Association under Bill Lavash had already retained me to debate the MCLU. The next day, the Massachusetts Civil Liberties Union called to say that they were cancelling the debate, since they felt it "would serve no constructive purpose". A day or so later, they also cancelled their legislation.

This was the death knell for what came to be known back then as "hollowpoint hysteria", but the bitter taste left in many police chiefs' mouths was so strong that they and their successors would avoid hollowpoint bullets like the plague.

The results would be written in blood. Every police department of any size that continued to issue non-hollowpoint bullets for the service .38 or the 9mm. or .38 would have stories the union patrolmen could tell you, stories of suspects taking multiple rounds and still shooting back, sometimes cutting down police officers. At this writing, the city fathers of Los Angeles have approved 9mm. automatics for the officers but still refuse to allow hollowpoints, despite numerous tests done by their own staff and brought in from outside that indicate the soft-nose bullets now issued in .38 and 9mm. are impotent man-stoppers.

San Diego PD was one of the "new breed" police agencies that focused strongly on public opinion, and for many years insisted their men carry round-nose lead .38 ammo. Only after so many officers had been killed in gunfights that San Diego won infamy as having more cops per capita murdered in the line of duty than anywhere else in America, and a task force was created to turn things around, did the department adopt hollowpoints for the issue .38 Special and the limited option 9mm. The rate of stopped felons on the street instantly soared, and at this writing, the 1,300-man department is looking seriously at adopting double-action 9mm. autoloaders with hollowpoints as issue for all personnel.

Yet many chiefs did not have the courage of Bill Kolender, the San

Diego chief who finally authorized hollowpoints, or Gene Gallagher, who was forced into soft noses by a city administration that feared the "dum-dum bullet spectre" in Indianapolis. After two of his officers were murdered by suspects who had taken multiple hits from their soft-nose-loaded .357 service revolvers, Gallagher defied the pols and issued 125-grain Magnum hollowpoints, effectively solving the problem. The next 10 shootings were 10 instant one-shot stops with no exit wounds.

If an agency finds it absolutely impossible for political reasons to go to hollowpoints, the one logical round is the .45 semiautomatic in military hardball configuration. The hollowpoint debates show for the record that those who wanted to ban "dum-dum" bullets *admitted* that regular police .38 ammo lacked stopping power, and ACLU indicated no problem with the cops going to the military style .45; after all, it was GI issue and "Geneva Convention approved".

.45 hardball is no worse in terms of ricochet and overpenetration than 158-grain lead round-nose .38 Special, is probably more controllable in stress shooting (the extra recoil of the .45 is more than compensated for by the automatic's much more manageable trigger pull), and stopping power of the 230-grain jacketed round-nose .45 is at par with the best 9mm. hollowpoints, and equal to or better than the best of the +P hollowpoint .38 Special cartridges.

Even in the 9mm., if one were stuck with old-fashioned round-nose ammo, it would still be better than the .38 Special, since the superior hit potential of the auto would drastically reduce the number of wild shots, hit potential would be greater and would therefore improve stopping probability; and accordingly, it is probable that officers with the 15-shot 9mm. pistols would have to fire fewer rounds to stop gunfights than those armed with 6-shot .38s.

Still, the fact remains that quality modern-design hollowpoints that have been proven on the street are by far the best choice for the police service and self defense semiautomatic pistol.

## Exotic Ammunition

By "Exotic Ammo" we mean ammunition that is unusually expensive and designed to perform specific functions through unique design features. There are numerous problems when considering such ammo for general self defense and police service purposes:

(a) The ammunition is extremely expensive; few departments or individuals can afford enough of this ammo for the standard test of "200 duty loads fired without malfunction" before one even begins to carry such ammo, let alone constant in-service training and qualification with it.

(b) The officer should never carry a round that can penetrate his own armor, in case his weapon is turned against him. Glasers in 9mm. and .357 (and special black-tip Glasers in virtually all calibers) can penetrate Level I and sometimes Level IIa armor, and BATS will consistently do so. Only because our officers wear Level IIa "Plus" Second Chance Y2+ body armor does my own department authorize the 9mm. BAT, which is just barely contained by this high level of protection.

(c) Exotic ammo is often virtually handmade and does not always have the quality control we associate with Federal, Remington, and Winchester.

(d) With little such ammo in the field, there is no significant real-world data base, except for Glaser and BAT ammo.

*Glaser Safety Slug.* This round, designed by the late Jack Canon, is a copper jacket "shell" filled with tiny #12 bird shot, capped at the front and driven at hypervelocity. My chronograph shows 1,400 feet per second for a Glaser .38 Special from a 2″ barrel, over 1,700 feet per second from .357 Magnum 4″. On impact, the nose begins to close in and about an inch and a half inside the flesh target, the projectile ruptures, spilling its high-velocity shot load at residual high velocity into the tissues.

The result is phenomenally destructive. In numerous shooting incidents studied involving people on the street, and personally observed with test animals in the abattoir, the writer has observed that this bullet always penetrates heavy bone and ruptures on the other side, creating absolutely devastating wounds. It almost never exits the body, almost never ricochets (hence the term "Safety Slug") and is extremely lethal.

The Glaser does, however, have certain shortcomings. Its penetration of intermediate barricade targets (tactical penetration) is satisfactory only if the bullet strikes on an absolutely straight-in angle that closes the bullet nose, giving the high-velocity projectile penetrative characteristics. With any significant angle of obliquity, the Glaser will disintegrate and fail to penetrate the intervening substance, in keeping with its "safety" designation. Side windows of automobiles have been known to defeat Glasers.

Also, the concept of penetrating 1.5 to 3″ and disintegrating does not translate if one has to shoot an opponent sideways. The human arm will effectively keep a Glaser from passing through and into the chest cavity, even though the arm may be torn to bits. I observed this in the autopsy that resulted from a fatal (multi-shot) Glaser .380 shooting in Miami.

We have seen many production runs of Glasers whose primers were not sealed against moisture or inclement weather. This can allow contaminating substances to seep into the cartridge case and render the cartridge useless.

Finally, and critically important with auto pistols, the Glaser round has a history of not working well in semiautomatics. Until late 1986, most production runs of Glasers had bullet shapes that did not feed well except in throated-out pistols. Also, the very light, very fast bullet has completely different recoil dynamics from conventional ball or hollow-point rounds. Recoil overall is generally less, and the pressure curve and peak pressure are not necessarily compatible with recoil-operated or gas-operated auto pistols designed to function with standard military and police loads. Often, particularly in 9mm. Parabellum and .380 calibers, the Glaser will run out of steam and fail to cycle the slide to feed the next cartridge into the chamber. This is particularly deceptive since most Glaser buyers are paying perhaps $15 or $20 for 6 cartridges out of their own pockets and will not actually fire them through the guns, instead hand-cycling the slide to "jack" the live rounds through the mechanism. Satisfied that the Glaser will feed, they don't realize it may not *cycle* and they might be carrying a single-shot pistol. The HK P7 pistol is notorious for this problem with Glasers, though it works superbly with conventional ammo.

A "new generation" of Glasers had been promised for well over a year before this manuscript was written, but has not yet materialized. The new Glaser will supposedly have a round nose for 100% feeding reliability, a different gunpowder for a more appropriate pressure curve for auto-pistol cycling, and the same terminal ballistic effect as the potent old Glaser. We are waiting, but not holding our breath.

Suffice to say that the Glaser is a very effective special-purpose round for the double-action revolver (stakeouts, home defense, sky marshal work and airline extradition, bailiff work, in short, any situation that requires maximum stopping power without shooting through intervening barricades, requires minimum penetration and ricochet, and can be accomplished with a revolver). For the auto, the author cannot recommend it at this time.

*The BAT Round.* In the late 1970s, the West German counterterrorist unit GSG-9 requested its government to come up with a 9mm. Parabellum cartridge suitable for both auto pistols and submachine guns that would stay inside the human body, give dramatic stopping power, deliver excellent tactical penetration, and still feed in military weapons designed only for the reliable cycling of ball ammunition.

Amazingly, the Government did so.

Geco, the West German ammo division of Dynamit-Nobel, came up with a 9mm. Luger cartridge originally called the GAS (Geco Action Safety) round. The U.S. importer gave it a most unfortunate name for public marketing purposes: the BAT (Blitz Action Trauma). Boxes of this ammo sold stateside usually bear the likeness of a vampire bat and, at one time, the U.S. importer's phone would be answered by a recorded announcement in a Dracula accent.

Widely touted in gun magazines as "the hot set-up for 9mm. Parabellum", this relatively expensive cartridge (about half the price of Glaser) was allegedly adopted by special units of FBI, Secret Service, and British SAS. Neither the manufacturer nor the distributor, however, could confirm any actual shootings of human beings with it. Meanwhile, our tests showed that it would (a) feed through any 9mm. Parabellum weapon that would feed hardball, including the Browning Hi-Power and every submachine gun tried; (b) travelled at over 1,400 feet per second out of a 4 " barrel; and (c) would penetrate Level I and sometimes Level IIa armor, stopping only in Level IIa Plus Second Chance. We fired the BAT, from a 5 " Browning pistol, through and through an Israeli ballistic helmet rated to stop the hot 9mm. NATO hardball round. In one side, out the other.

Still, we were skeptical, since no actual shootings had been documented. However, a trip to Venezuela to train police in 1985 filled out the data base. While teaching under the auspices of senior members of DISIP, Venezuela's internal security police, I learned that their SWAT teams and heavy duty felony response units used the BAT in their Browning pistols and Uzi and Mini-Uzi submachine guns. I was given access to some 73 documented gunshot wounds with the GAS/BAT round, most with submachine guns but including at least six with the 5 " barrel pistol.

**None** of the bullets had exited, except for peripheral hits that were glancing wounds. **All** bullets had opened in the standard BAT pattern and stayed inside the body. **All** perpetrators had gone down instantly after being shot. Survival rate was very low.

One X-ray showed a typically expanded BAT slug in the midst of a human thoracic vertebra. The vertebra resembled a fistful of matchsticks; it had been "shivered" vertically, something I have never seen even with high-power rifle wounds. The standard pattern of the BAT bullet — a solid brass projectile with a deep hollow cavity that is filled by a plastic insert to create a round-nose cartridge shape for good feeding — is for the plastic nose cap to be blown off as soon as the projectile leaves the muzzle. The now cup-pointed slug strikes, still spinning from the rifling. As the hollow cavity fills with flesh, its thin walls peel back into flat, sharp-edged fingers that slice like a fan as the bullet passes through soft tissue and, typically, half of those "fingers" will shear off during passage, sometimes more, sometimes less. The result is a significant wound and excellent stopping characteristics. When hard barricade material is encountered, the hard brass edges of the brass bullet tend to bite in like a cookie cutter, ripping through and hitting like a flat-nose wadcutter when the bullet finally encounters flesh.

The writer furnished BAT ammo to his chief of police, who carried a short-barrel S&W model 669 duty pistol. In two shootings of animals, he was quite impressed. An injured deer that had to be humanely destroyed was shot with the BAT at close range, and the side of its head exploded outward, with no actual bullet exit. A pit bull coming at the Chief was shot in the center of the forehead and stopped instantly: finger-thick jets of blood and cerebrospinal fluid were observed to spurt from both ears. Seconds after the animal had collapsed and died from the immediate stop, a witness shouted, "My God, what did you *hit* him with?" The bullet had lodged safely inside the skull.

Specifically designed for counterterrorist use and minimum danger to innocent persons, the BAT round is eminently court defensible when used in the police service. It would be best, however, to avoid the inflammatory American terminology and refer to the cartridge by its proper European designation: GAS, or Geco Action Safety, round.

## Summary

At this writing, the author would recommend the following ammunition for police service semiautomatic pistols:

.380: Winchester Silvertip (warning: most pistols must be throated by the armorer). The special-purpose MMP (Maximum Medium Pistol) round, sort of a Mini-BAT, gives similar performance and will feed in any .380 that feeds ball ammo, but is more expensive and less street-proven in actual shootings.

9mm. Parabellum: Federal 115-grain JHP designated "9BP". For special units or select budget officers, the Geco Action Safety (BAT) round. Federal will feed in SIG, Beretta, and third generation S&W service pistols, BAT in any weapon that feeds ball ammo. Second choice: third generation Winchester Silvertip. For the department issuing numerous older model 9mm. pistols: Remington 115-grain jacketed hollowpoint.

.45 ACP: Speer 200-grain JHP if issue weapon is S&W 645 or SIG P-220. Federal post-'86 185-grain hollowpoint for any other recent model .45 automatic. If weapons include WWI and WWII vintage, and early commercial .45 automatics, the Remington 185-grain JHP.

.38 Super: Sufficient data base does not exist, but officers carrying this weapon might be well advised to use Remington 115-grain .38 Super if gun has not been throated, Winchester Silvertip .38 Super if feed

*S&W's aluminum alloy frame model 439 proved with the Illinois State Police that the special +P+ 9mm. Parabellum load was a decisive manstopper that would work reliably on modern auto pistols. Now available from Winchester and Remington, that round is a 115-grain jacketed hollowpoint loaded to nearly 1400 feet per second velocity from a 4" barrel pistol.*

ramp has been widened and polished.

It is respectfully suggested that hardball or full metal jacket (FMJ) non-hollowpoint bullets **not** be issued in **any** caliber, due to danger of overpenetration and ricochet, and reduced stopping power capability.

*Though theoretically promising, the 10mm. cartridge as used in Bren Ten and Colt Delta Elite (shown) is unproven in the field, and some believe it may be dangerously overpenetrative. Author does not recommend it for street use at this time.*

*If for political or regulation reasons a department must issue military-style "Geneva Convention" ammo, .45 auto 230-grain hardball is the most effective such round available, though author doesn't feel this or any such cartridge is suitable for police service. SIG P-220 shown has 8-round .45 capacity.*

However, if the agency is forbidden to use hollowpoints or required to use Geneva Convention/military style ammunition, the 230-grain full metal jacket .45 Auto is clearly the cartridge of choice.

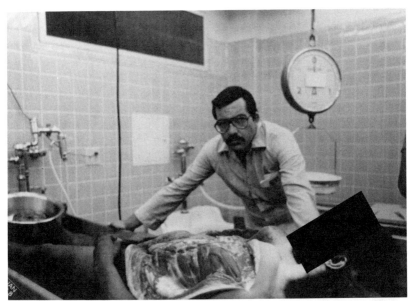

*There's only one way to find out how police bullets work in the real world. Author is shown at autopsy of shooting victim. Recommendations in text are based on bullet performance in actual gunfights.*

# DUTY LEATHER FOR THE SERVICE AUTOLOADER

Since auto pistols are relatively new to the police equipment scene, there are fewer models of holsters and ammo carriers available for them than for revolvers. At the same time, due to the slightly greater complexity of design, holster selection for the auto pistol must be made more carefully.

Since the typical police holster will have a safety strap going over the hammer area, it is imperative that the pistol not be equipped with an oversized safety catch. The leather strap can fit it too tightly, sometimes causing the safety to be moved from the "on safe" to the "off safe" position by the taut leather.

If a thumb-release safety strap is used, the officer should learn to thumb the release paddle directly inward toward the body. Otherwise, the end of the safety strap can become entangled between his thumb and the slide of the pistol, jamming the weapon into the holster when he needs it quickly in a panic situation.

The best spare magazine carriers take two forms. Open-top carriers with friction-retaining devices allow the fastest access to the spare magazines, but also expose part of the magazine to the elements. Flapped carriers protect somewhat better, but are much slower to draw from. This writer generally carries one open-topped Snick carrier in front of the left hip for fast access and a Velcro-flapped Safariland single pouch behind the left hip for backup. This assures that a fall or struggle that might dislodge a magazine from the open-top carrier still leaves at least one magazine secured on the belt and always accessible. In a high-risk situation, there will be a Bianchi Clip-Grip open-topped, friction-screw double carrier at the left hip, with a flapped Bianchi Piggyback behind it. The Piggyback carrier is thick, but takes up only the width of one magazine on the duty belt and served me superbly for many years as the only ammo carrier for my uniform duty Colt .45 auto.

Other excellent magazine carriers are produced by Milt Sparks, G. Wm. Davis Leather, and Ted Blocker. Tex Shoemaker also offers a superb auto leather line.

I believe the best of the thumb-break holsters are the "Usher" style, developed originally by G. Wm. Davis for Jerry Usher when he was a cop in Southern California. Steel plates reinforce the holster, and a rubber roller friction-secures on the frame in front of the trigger guard. The officer can instantly reholster his gun one-handed, by feel, and if he has to run and traverse obstacles before he can refasten the safety strap, the friction roller holds the gun very secure. The classic, original "Gordon" Davis model 4500 holster is an excellent choice for duty. I wear my .45 auto in one, cut to 1¾ " belt slot width for the Garrison belt when in the administrative uniform. Similar designs by Milt Sparks and Ted Blocker are likewise excellent, and Viking Leather offers an acceptable low-priced version.

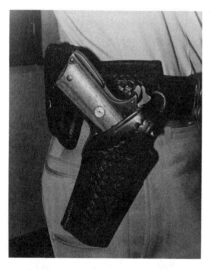

*Colt 1911-pattern or Browning P-35 is properly carried cocked and locked. When gun is visible to the public, there should be a safety strap between hammer and firing pin as on this Safariland holster for Colt Mk. IV .45 which was standard issue for many years with El Monte, California, police department.*

Snatch-resistant holsters have always been more difficult to design for autos than for revolvers. It is easy to build niches in the holster that cling to the back of a cylinder or the recurve of a revolver's trigger guard. The streamlined, flat-sided auto pistol is more challenging to holster designers.

For many years this writer carried his .45 auto in a Bucheimer-Clark Police Auto Breakfront, the first such holster for the police auto. This was not a security holster, but the option of drawing through the front when seated in the patrol car or through the top when standing made it my duty rig of choice. I later switched to the Bianchi AutoDraw, which cost more than $100,000 to develop. It secured with a plastic lock inside the trigger guard, requiring the officer to push down and then forward.

The famous weapon retention and disarming instructor John Peters was unable to disarm me despite some ten seconds of nonresistance when we tested this rig, and when he finally found the "combination", I was able to easily retain the weapon using one of John's own techniques.

Since the holster did not have a jacket cut and was open-bottomed (a design poorly suited to winter patrol in Northern New England, where an officer can easily plug his gun muzzle if he kneels to examine evidence in the snow while wearing an open-bottom holster), I wore it only in the summer. In the winter I continued to carry the Bucheimer-Clark, which had a closed bottom and jacket cut.

The newer version of the Bucheimer Auto Breakfront introduced in the mid-1980s is a better all-around duty holster. It has a trigger guard retaining device similar to the autodraw, with the closed bottom and jacket cut of its predecessor's design. It is also easier to draw from than the Bianchi security holster, which requires considerable practice on the part of the officer.

In the mid-80s, Bill Rogers of Rogers Leather designed a superb duty holster shortly before his firm merged with Safariland Leather. The Rogers SS-III holster was so named because it provided safety and security with three different features. First was the conventional thumb-break safety strap over the hammer area. Second was another strap that went behind the trigger guard and was released by the tip of the officer's middle finger during the drawing motion. Third was a design feature that required the pistol to be rocked back at a certain angle to clear the holster at all.

*Author believes Rogers SS-III is best police uniform security holster for auto pistols on the market at this time. It does, however, require considerable training. It is shown with S&W 645.*

When the holster was shown at the Bianchi Cup tournament, I volunteered to try it, and strapped it on with a Smith & Wesson model 659 auto in place. I released both safety straps. Dick Crawford, the NRA referee and famous shooter who stands some 6'5" tall, was able to pick me bodily off the ground holding only the butt of the S&W auto, but the gun never came out of the holster. I was impressed. The SS-III is probably the most secure holster now offered for duty auto or revolver, but the user should be cautioned that it also requires more practice than any other holster if the officer wearing it is to be able to draw it smoothly in a fast-reaction situation.

Given the different missions and skill levels of different officers, it makes sense to give them several options of holsters the department has approved. This approach has worked well with LAPD, which over the years allowed four or five approved holsters to be carried by the officers, resulting in high confidence and performance levels that helped LAPD lead the nation in percentage of hits with their revolvers in actual gunfights. Such a policy may be even more important with the duty autoloader, which will be new to some of the troops and more difficult to get used to. In the writer's own department, a variety of duty holsters, mostly high-ride, forward tilt thumb-breaks, are in use by the officers carrying autoloaders in uniform.

*Hi-ride holster is contra-indicated for female officers: shorter torso combined with higher pelvis puts this SIG P-226's butt near the officer's shoulder blade. Policewomen will work better with lower-riding holsters such as a Border Patrol with properly curved shank.*

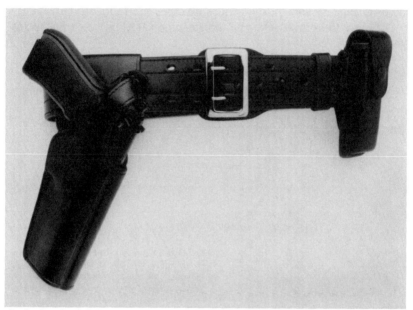

*Border Patrol style holster carries better for females and many males as well. This complete duty rig for Beretta 92F is by Bianchi. Bianchi photo.*

When selecting holsters, it is important that the trigger guard area of the gun be covered. The primary reason for this is that, in a struggle, a suspect who gets his hands on the officer's gun can fire a shot while it is still in the holster if he can get at the trigger.

A secondary reason for the covered trigger guard, often erroneously given as the primary reason, is to prevent an officer accidentally shooting himself on the draw if the pistol snags as he is withdrawing it with his finger on the trigger. This is particularly likely to happen with a single-action auto if the officer has erroneously released the safety while beginning the draw.

However, what goes up must come down, and what is drawn must be reholstered. With the current generation of police auto holsters with covered trigger guards, a major pattern of accidental discharge that has emerged is accidental shooting while reholstering. Typically, an under-trained or careless officer will be attempting to holster with the finger still on the trigger and will have neglected to decock the pistol or activate the safety. As the gun goes into the holster, the trigger finger stops and the gun keeps going. The trigger is driven against the finger, and a shot goes into the officer's leg.

To prevent this, officers should be taught the "LFI method" of

reholstering. As shown, the officer executes the following procedure:
1) Before the gun reaches the holster, the safety is "on" and/or the gun is decocked.
2) The trigger finger is extended straight forward outside the trigger guard.
3) The thumb is placed on the hammer, holding it down on a double-action or back on a single-action pistol.

*The LFI method of one-handed holstering prevents accidental discharges at that point. Thumb holds hammer in proper position, index finger is clear of trigger guard and "points" weapon into scabbard. Note that muzzle is inserted at rear of holster, then slide is rocked forward, clearing safety strap. SIG P-220 .45 and LFI Concealment Rig are shown.*

This prevents accidental shootings first by keeping the finger out of the trigger guard, second by preventing the hammer from falling (single action) or rising and falling (double action) should the trigger be activated. In the case of the Colt 1911 type pistol, it also pulls the web of the hand away from the grip safety, so that part can do its work and keep the gun from going off.

There are also special concerns with off-duty and plainclothes holsters for the auto pistol, but nothing that can't be taken care of with some simple policies. Concealment holsters should be rigidly reinforced to allow one-handed reholstering by feel. That tactic is vital to the officer who is about to handcuff a suspect, or who knows that after he has taken command of a scene at the point of his weapon, responding officers who don't know him by sight could mistake him for a "man with a gun" if his sidearm was not in the holster upon their arrival. Soft, floppy holsters that ride inside the waistband and secure only with fragile metal clips should be forbidden. Most top manufacturers have excellent inside-the-waistband holsters that allow positive draw and easy reholstering. These include the #3 from Bianchi, the LFI concealment rig from Ted Blocker, and the classic Summer Special from Bruce Nelson, Milt Sparks, and other makers. The best low-priced unit is probably the Talon by Alessi.

*When inside the waistband holster is not comfortable for plainclothes wear, an excellent choice is a hi-ride scabbard like this RoadRunner by Milt Sparks Leather. It carries the author's Colt Commander .45, modified with improved grip safety, ambidextrous thumb safety, and Wilson hi-visibility sights.*

Upside-down holsters can only hold the flat-sided auto pistol with a safety strap, and if the strap comes loose, the gun falls to the ground. This can be fatal if the pistol is a Browning Hi-Power, first or second generation S&W 9mm., or pre-Series '80 Colt auto. Upside-down and horizontal shoulder holsters, in this writer's opinion, should be forbidden for use with such guns. There are numerous excellent shoulder holsters such as the Bianchi X-15 that work fine with such weapons.

Each officer should be encouraged to carefully mate his holster with his weapon. In the early days of the S&W auto pistol's use in American law enforcement, an officer armed with a model 39 was severely slashed. As he drew his gun and pulled the trigger on the knife man who was coming at him, nothing happened: the long magazine release button had hit the unyielding leather of his Bucheimer duty holster, causing the magazine to fall out and activate the magazine disconnector safety. S&W responded by shortening the length of the mag release button, and

Bucheimer (and other smart makers) reacted by making a cut-out in the holster shank in the area where the mag release button might have otherwise contacted. In 1986, a police department issued a warning on teletype when they learned that their issue Beretta 92 SBF semiautomatics would disassemble themselves when inserted a certain way in one model of tight-fitting Safariland shoulder holster.

Those officers who carry cocked and locked semiautomatics are often concerned about the appearance of the weapon in the holster. Some people are alarmed by the very thought of a cocked gun being carried, ignoring the fact that virtually all hunting rifles and shotguns, and similar weapons used by police, are also cocked and locked in normal carry. The pistol, however, has an exposed hammer that calls attention to the situation, unlike the discreet internal-hammer designs of weapons like the AR-15, the Mini-14, and the generic police slide-action shotgun.

In several years of carrying the semiautomatic Colt Government Model or equivalent Condition One in uniform, this writer received only two comments. One was from a police lieutenant who carried a double-action auto pistol himself, but was shocked to see one of his patrolmen carrying a pistol with the hammer back. After a long lecture on why John Browning had designed the pistol to be carried just this way, the lieutenant was unmoved. All he had to say was, "It still scares me." I replied, "Don't feel bad; it's normal to be frightened of things you don't understand." Altogether not the most politic remark of my police career.

The only "citizen" to comment on it unfavorably was a suspect I had just arrested for illegal possession of a concealed weapon. As the handcuffed individual was being helped into the patrol car, he sneered, "What do *you* know about guns? I bet you didn't even know your own gun is cocked in its holster right now!" I smiled as I secured the suspect behind the cage and replied something like, "I certainly appreciate your firearms expertise, sir." I was on the state champion police combat pistol team at the time, and the pistol was a Colt National Match .45 autoloader, cocked and locked.

Trivial though the problem was, I was able to solve it by taking a "hammer shield", the little bat-wing shaped piece of leather sold by Don Hume to cover the raspy hammer spur of a Smith & Wesson revolver and keep it from cutting up the uniform jacket, and putting it backwards on the safety strap of my .45 holster. In that position, it not only completely covered the hammer and kept anyone from seeing whether the hammer was cocked, but also shielded the vulnerable open firing pin area of my cocked Colt from rain and snow. It never slowed down my draw with the Bucheimer Police Auto Breakfront holster, but conceivably might with other designs. An officer using this trick of the trade should perform several practice speed draws with the unloaded service weapon before carrying this holster attachment on duty.

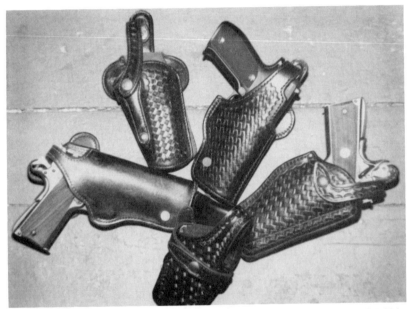

*Good choices are, clockwise from 12: Hi-ride thumbbreak by Ted Blocker (shown w/SIG P-226); Bucheimer Auto Breakfront for Colt .45 has strap between hammer and firing pin for safety even when safety is disengaged as shown; Rogers SS-III (shown for S&W m/659) is most popular auto security holster; G. Wm. Davis model 4500, shown with combat-customized Springfield Armory 1911-AI, was designed by Jerry Usher; Bianchi AutoDraw was first hi-security police auto rig.*

# TACTICAL AND SPEED RELOADING OF THE SEMIAUTOMATIC PISTOL

One of the autoloader's long-heralded advantages is its speed of reloading. The very best combat shooters can reload a semiautomatic in a second or less, versus between two and three seconds for the same Combat Masters to speedload a revolver. Working with average line officers, weapons training authority John Farnam discovered that the practical time limit was three seconds to reload the semiautomatic versus six seconds to do it with a six-gun and speedloaders. If the revolver is not backed up by speedloaders, and instead its wearer has to reload from dump pouches or individual shell loops, the task is likely to take the better part of ten seconds.

## The Speed Reload

If only one method of reloading is to be taught the officer, it should be the Speed Reload. It is accomplished as follows:

1) Holding the gun on target with the strong hand, the officer grabs a fresh magazine with the weak hand.

2) Keeping the gun's grip perpendicular with the ground, the officer presses the magazine release, ejecting the depleted "clip".

3) Pulling the gun somewhat closer to the body and turning the butt toward the weak hand, while still keeping the muzzle somewhat on target, the officer inserts the fresh magazine into the butt of the pistol.

4) The officer forcibly slaps the magazine all the way in, and as the fingers of the support hand come back to their two-handed position on the gun, the weak hand hits the slide release *whether or not* the slide is locked back. Photos show the proper sequence.

Why do the fingers hit the slide release even when the slide is already in the forward (released) position? This is "fail-safe" training. In an actual gunfight, when the officer's attention may be focused forward on the danger or where it may be too dark to see if the slide has locked back or not, the officer wants his hands programmed to automatically release the slide if the gun has run completely dry. Pressing the slide

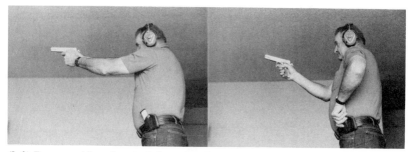

(Left) Former world combat pistol champ Ray Chapman demonstrates Speed Reload of service auto. Pistol is stainless Colt Government .45. (Right) Don't wait until pistol is empty to reload. With at least one round still in gun, Chapman removes finger from trigger and pulls gun slightly in toward him as weak hand drops to mag pouch. Weak hand palm touches floorplate, thumb and forefinger grasp magazine. Notice that previous magazine, which may still contain rounds, is not ejected until fresh magazine has been indexed.

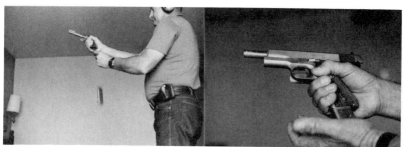

(Left) As fresh mag is brought up to gun, depleted one is ejected by thumb of gun hand. Left-handed officer would use middle or index finger to hit button release. (Right) Magazine is firmly seated into pistol. In this photo, gun has been run dry to slidelock; thumb of either hand can trip slide release to activate pistol as soon as fresh magazine is slapped home.

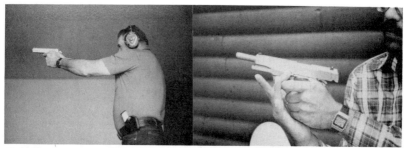

(Left) Shooter returns to firing position. (Right) Author demonstrates slide release technique for left-handed shooter: middle finger of weak hand activates release as hand goes from slapping in magazine back to firing position. Right-handed man would ideally use left thumb at the same point.

release when the slide is forward does no harm and takes the smallest fraction of a second to accomplish.

In theory, the officer should keep count of his rounds and always have one cartridge in the chamber when he reloads; this allows him to merely swap magazines, a quicker procedure than changing mags *and* dropping the slide. However, real-world street experience shows that an officer so trained will almost certainly lose count of his shots in a real gun battle. When training takes over, he is likely to change magazines and keep pulling the trigger futilely, because he has not been trained to reload from a worst-case-scenario slidelock. This is why at least half of reloading training should be from full slidelock, and in the rest of the training, the officer should be encouraged to automatically hit the slide release as he completes the loading process.

## The Tactical Reload

Between the two World Wars, German small arms doctrine changed from the speed reload to the battlefield reload. In the speed reload, the spent magazine is jettisoned, while in the battlefield reload, the partially depleted magazine is retained on the person to be refilled later. This change in philosophy was reflected in changing German service pistol design. While the Luger of WWI had the same type of side-button magazine release as the Colt-Browning style used on most service pistols in the U.S., it was replaced by the Walther P-38 with butt-heel magazine release catch. The latter design forced the soldier to remove the spent clip and presumably put it in his pocket or webbing.

Since this made for a somewhat slower reload, some U.S. handgun authorities opined that it showed a Teutonic disregard for human life: "Imagine placing more value on a five-dollar magazine than on a soldier's life!" On the contrary, the Germans were well aware of the priorities for their men's long term survival. Most soldiers are issued only the pistol and two or three magazines. If all those magazines are left in the mud as the soldier reloads on the run, he may have won the battle but lost the war: when the encounter is over, he has no more magazines to load into his pistol for the *next* fight. In wartime, the service pistol usually takes the same cartridge as the force's submachine gun, so *cartridges* in that caliber to reload the magazines will be in plentiful supply. However, since the pistol itself has a relatively low priority on the ordnance list, extra handgun magazines will be hard to come by.

The first to see the value of this military concept for police use was SWAT weapons expert Chuck Taylor, who called the technique "The Tactical Reload" and promulgated its use in this country. Taylor also refined the technique to a fast and positive reloading method. While many imitators have attempted to come up with a better tactical reload, most gain better handling of the depleted magazine at the expense of weakening the hand's hold on the fresh one. Since the magazine we can afford to drop in this complicated process is obviously the partly spent one that we might have been prepared to completely dump anyway, positive hold on the full mag should not be sacrificed. This is one of two reasons I prefer the Taylor technique. The other is that in this method, the officer will initially grasp the spare magazine exactly the way he would in a speed reload. Thus we have commonality of training, and the officer does not have to learn a separate grasp of the fresh magazine.

The Taylor-type tactical reload is accomplished as follows:

1) Grasp the spare magazine with the weak hand, just as would be done in a speed reload. The partially loaded pistol is kept on target.

2) As the hands come together, the weak hand holding the fresh mag turns its palm upward under the pistol's butt.

3) The partially depleted magazine is ejected, its floorplate being caught by the palm of the waiting weak hand. Little finger and ring finger encircle the body of the partially depleted magazine and remove it from the pistol.

4) The hand rolls slightly to the side and slaps the fresh magazine into the butt, just as it would during a speed reload. The gun returns forward to cover the danger zone.

5) The partially depleted magazine is stored somewhere on the person for later access.

*Author demonstrates Tactical Reload with SIG P-226 9mm. Trigger finger leaves guard, pistol comes in toward the body at 45° high ready position as weak hand grasps spare magazine in same hold as for Speed Reload.*

*Thumb and middle finger hold magazine as rest of hand opens under gun butt. Partly spent magazine is ejected into the waiting palm.*

*Little finger and ring finger lock partly depleted magazine as hand rolls over slightly and inserts the full magazine as in Speed Reload.*

*Fresh magazine is slapped in place. Since by definition Tactical Reload is done only on gun that is still partly loaded, release of slide is not part of procedure.*

*Partly loaded magazine is now returned to pocket, waistband, or pouch. If latter, place it in backward so hand will be able to tell it from full magazine when it touches.*

What value has this technique, designed for soldiers on a battlefront, to domestic police? While the officer may not be 5,000 miles from his homeland and base line of supply, being caught on a lonely road without backup in a gunfight with a vanload of outlaws is close enough. If the situation deteriorates into a high volume of fire, the typical officer with only two reloads on his belt may need every single cartridge. Thus, a partially spent magazine with three rounds in it could be the only thing that saves him from death a few minutes later.

Taylor suggests that the partially depleted magazine be placed in a pocket, so the officer won't reach for his belt and mistake a half-used "clip" for a fresh one. On the other hand, the officer is not trained to reach to his pocket for a spare magazine. This writer prefers to return the partly depleted magazine to the belt pouch, but *backwards*. Now, if the hands should reflexively reach for it, the palm feels the sharp edge of the backward floorplate and realizes, "Whoa, last-ditch suicide magazine" in time to move on to a full mag that is in its proper place. Either technique is acceptable, and the officer should use what comes naturally to him or her.

Some have gone so far as to recommend that the tactical reload be taught exclusively, and the speed reload dropped. I profoundly disagree. One authority who makes that suggestion cites the common and erroneous figure of 2.3 rounds being fired per participant per gunfight, and states that he is unaware of a situation in which officers ever had to reload in a gunfight. On the contrary, a significant percentage of NYPD officers have reloaded in the midst of gun battles, and in shootouts from Texas to California, some cops have had to reload twice in the heat of running gunfights. For such a problem, the speed reload is the obvious answer. The tactical reload is at its best when the officer is ensconced behind cover and facing a prolonged siege-type gunfight against multiple opponents.

This writer believes that if only one reloading method is taught, it should be the speed reload. If there is a lull in the action after the reload, the officer can always reach down and retrieve the partially loaded magazine. If time permits, the tactical reload is a very useful special purpose and auxiliary technique to add to the officer's repertoire.

One reason for the tactical reload's newfound popularity is that it is handy for training: magazines are not being dumped and getting scratched or dirty on the range. This, however, was the rationale years ago when rangemasters forced officers to dump their revolver brass into their pockets before reloading. That nicety and convenience cost officers their lives, because it programmed them to stuff useless brass into their pockets

*A line of shooters practice reloading during auto pistol class at Lethal Force Institute.*

in desperate moments when a second saved in reloading could have meant the difference between life and death. Classic examples include the death of Officer Pence in the Newhall Massacre, and an incident related by the legendary Border Patrolman Bill Jordan in his excellent book "No Second Place Winner".

The problem with the tactical reload is that it can be fumble-prone under stress, and takes too much time if the officer is in immediate, continued danger. The technique's inventor, Chuck Taylor, estimates four seconds are consumed in a tactical reload, yet Taylor himself can execute a speed reload in a second. A method that takes four times as long can get one killed in a fast-breaking situation. Hence the recommendation that the speed reload be taught first, the tactical reload taught second as an option if time permits.

It will be noted in auto pistol training that dropping an empty magazine on asphalt usually will not damage it other than cosmetically. However, dropping a fully loaded magazine on a hard surface can cause its sheet metal walls to rupture, since there is much greater impact due to the weight of the cartridges inside. Even an empty magazine can be filled with grit and lose reliability if dropped often enough on loose dirt or in sand. It is an excellent idea to lay plastic sheets or tarpaulins in front of the firing line during auto pistol training to prevent this. The sheeting will also save time when policing spent brass.

# CLEARING MALFUNCTIONS

Modern hi-tech auto pistols are extraordinarily reliable with good-quality factory ammunition. The most malfunction-free handgun under abuse this writer has seen is the HK P7 9mm. autoloader.

Yet the fact remains that anything made by man can fail. The good news is that a jammed autoloader is generally much quicker to get back into action than a jammed revolver. Designed to be self-cycled, the autoloader lends itself to manipulation that quickly gets defective cartridges out of the way; the revolver that seizes up often needs a skilled gunsmith to bring it back to firing condition.

*Old-fashioned "thumb crossover" grip still taught by many police academies was poor even with revolvers, since thumb could slip upward and block hammer, jamming the sixgun. With autos, a thumb that rides too high or has an unaccustomed thick glove on it can block the slide, injuring the thumb and jamming the pistol. The thumb should ride low and to the side when firing the combat semiautomatic pistol.*

The most common malfunctions, and the most effective responses to them, are as follows:

*Failure to go into battery* is diagnosed when the slide has not gone all the way forward. In most cases, the gun can be brought back into action by maintaining a firing hold with the strong hand, finger clear of trigger, and slapping the back of the slide sharply with the heel of the weak hand's palm.

*Slide fails to return to battery. This is general-ly due to a dirty gun or a weakly held pistol.*

*Failure to return to battery can generally be cured by slapping the back of the slide sharply forward with a palm-heel strike by the weak hand.*

*Smokestack jam* occurs most commonly when there is too weak a car-tridge in the chamber, or too weak a hold on the pistol when it is fired. In the latter case, part of the recoil impulse transmits through the frame into the unlocked wrist. When this happens, recoil momentum dissipates before it can finish working the slide, and the spent case is not rammed hard enough against the ejector. As a result, the spent case is caught inside the ejection port of the slide, sticking upward, hence the term "smokestack".

Several dangerously incorrect methods of responding to this malfunc-tion have been taught in the past. One is to pull back the slide in "slingshot" fashion and attempt to shake the shell loose. This can, however, cause the spent casing to fall back into the mechanism, com-pounding instead of clearing the malfunction. Others have suggested sweeping back the weak hand across the top of the slide, with the web of the hand toward the shooter. This can occasionally trap the spent round inside the slide, and in any case will often cause the palm to be lacerated in training. A technique that imparts pain to the student in training is a technique he will be dangerously hesitant with on the street.

The author prefers the following technique to clear a smokestack. The strong hand takes finger off trigger and holds gun rigidly toward the target. The weak hand comes up and with the heel of the palm—an in-sensitive "body weapon"—rakes along the top of the slide and carries through as it contacts the smokestacked shell casing. The casing is flung clear and the slide is racked by the same motion, allowing the gun to cycle again. No significant pain or injury is imparted to the shooter and the casing cannot be trapped in the ejection port. The technique is ex-ecuted as a karate chop to the shooting-arm's shoulder.

*Smokestack is a common malfunction, typically caused by underpowered round, extremely dirty gun, or weak hold on the pistol.*

*To clear, bring heel of weak hand back across slide like a karate chop until it engages the smokestacked empty casing.*

*Continue "karate chop" movement toward shoulder of firing arm. This drags the spent casing and the slide back until the case snaps clear and the slide snaps forward, chambering the next live round. The pistol is now ready to fire again. Shown is Lt. Robert D'Allesandro with his duty S&W 659 9mm. Jam clearing drills should be a part of all police auto pistol training programs.*

*Double Feed* is perhaps the trickiest jam to clear. It occurs from extraction failure: the spent, fired case is left in the chamber and as the slide cycles, the next live round is rammed into the head of the jammed case.

In most cases the slide will be holding the fresh cartridge halfway in the feed lips of the magazine, preventing a gravity drop of the magazine.

Simply working the slide will allow another cartridge to come up against the spent one, and the first may also be caught there. Thus, merely working the slide will aggravate rather than clear the jam.

*Double-feed caused by ejection failure is the most difficult of the common malfunctions to clear. No standard "all around" jam clearing technique will relieve this stoppage. Spent casing is still in chamber, and fresh cartridge that was next up in magazine has stopped against it, half in and half out of the magazine's feed lips, and under strong tension from the spring-loaded slide.*

*To clear double feed, first run slide all the way back with weak hand and push up slide lock. If slide is not locked back, forward tension will prevent trapped magazine from clearing gun.*

*Rip magazine out of gun. The topmost cartridge will have moved too far forward to reliably feed again and may even have smokestacked inside the feed lips; for this reason, the magazine that was in the gun should be thrown to the ground.*

*Slide is then operated several times (if in the dark) or until the spent casing that caused the problem has been ejected.*

*Spare magazine is now grabbed from belt pouch. The possibility of a double feed jam, which requires a second magazine to remedy, is one reason why at least one spare mag should be carried by all officers on or off duty, even those with high capacity magazines like this 659.*

*Fresh magazine is inserted smartly into butt of pistol.*

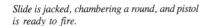

*Slide is jacked, chambering a round, and pistol is ready to fire.*

The indicated response to this difficult malfunction is: (1) Manually bring the slide to the rear and lock it by thumbing up the slide stop. (2) Remove the magazine, which is now no longer under tension and should come away freely. (3) Jettison the removed magazine: the top round has been moved out of proper position and may even now be standing vertical with the case rim trapped between the feed lips. It will not reliably function if reinserted. (4) Work the slide rapidly with a slingshot hold until the spent casing has been ejected. (5) Insert fresh magazine, jack slide, fire as necessary.

*Failure to Fire* is typically caused by one of two things: a bad cartridge or a magazine that has not been fully inserted and cannot bring its cartridges up high enough for the slide to strip into the chamber. Whichever the problem is, it is solved by the military "tap-rack-bang" drill. (1) *Tap.* The floorplate of the magazine is sharply slapped with the weak hand to make sure it is now in position. (2) *Rack.* The slide is jacked smartly to the rear, ejecting the defective cartridge and/or chambering a fresh one. (3) *Bang.* Firing continues.

*Short-gripped Colt Officer's Model, furnished with 6-shot magazine, will accept 7-shot magazine from larger 1911 and Government Model pistols. However, when shoved in hard after pistol has been run to slidelock, the longer magazine may over travel and jam, locking slide to the rear. Clearing technique is to press in on magazine release button with gun hand thumb, draw D-Jammer tool or similar object from belt or pocket, and ram it down through ejection port to punch magazine out. Close slide, reload with fresh magazine, jack the slide to chamber a round, and continue firing.*

Competency in worst-case scenarios demands that each person carrying the auto pistol have practiced jam-clearing under controlled conditions. Remember in training that it will damage the magazines if they are dropped on hard ground while loaded, and that after being dropped in sand or dirt, they should be disassembled and cleaned.

# SELECTING THE AUTOLOADER FOR POLICE SERVICE AND SELF-DEFENSE

Carrying police autoloaders since 1973 and having been able to tap into the experiences of the U.S. military police, Illinois State Police, LAPD, Las Vegas Metro, and uncounted other agencies with extensive law enforcement duty experience with the semiautomatic, this writer believes that certain procedures and policies should accompany the adoption or approval of such weapons.

There should definitely be input from the rank and file officers who will be trusting their lives to the gun. Illinois State Police, with the first great experiment in the domestic police service automatic, for more than a decade suffered a morale problem with troopers who, in my survey conducted through their FOP lodge in 1977, overwhelmingly rated themselves as less than totally confident with the 9mm. Smith & Wesson. First, they had been given a gun not yet proven, that would go through two more generations of development, developments largely instigated by the experiences of ISP itself, before the gun's technology reached acceptable levels of reliability in this writer's opinion. Second, the decision to switch from "any Colt or Smith & Wesson .38 or .357 revolver" to the mandatory Model 39 struck the 1,700 road troopers as an arbitrary decision made by the head of ordnance and the commandant, and forced down their unwilling throats. It would take more than a decade (and a new gun, the improved third generation model 439) before the majority of the officers would be comfortable and confident with the weapon.

The department should understand that the history of the autoloader in the police service shows that, while overall performance will improve markedly and there will be a dramatic improvement in the shooting scores of what had been the poorest marksmen with the revolver, there will be an early period where the previous top revolver shooters drop somewhat in their scores until they have mastered the new pistol. This naturally causes them negative feelings which, understandably, they project onto the new gun. The top shots on the force are powerful opinion makers among the rank and file, and if the men perceived as the precinct's gun experts say the new duty weapon is junk, it's no wonder that a lot of the other troops will be influenced by their opinion.

*Human engineering and compatibility with officers should be examined before issuing new autos. S&W 9mm.s initially got a bad rap from Illinois State Troopers because they felt an untried new gun had been foisted on them by management edict; author feels transition would have gone smoother if field troopers had had input to the change. Ayoob is shown with test Ruger P-85 and rapid fire target.*

*Accuracy testing is a critical factor. Studies show that when departments convert to autos, poorer shooters improve significantly, overall proficiency increases noticeably, but scores of the very top shooters drop temporarily until they acclimate to the gun. Because the best shots on the force influence the opinion of other officers, they should know the accuracy capability of the new auto from the beginning. Here, a 10mm. Colt Delta Elite recoils in its Ransom Rest as Ray Chapman tests its 50-yard accuracy. Pistol shot excellent 3" groups with Norma brand ammo.*

Thus, the precinct and district firearms instructors and those identified by records as the top shots on the force should be invited to participate in the testing process when adoption of any new gun, including the semiautomatic service pistol, is considered. Accuracy testing on sandbags or machine rests will prove that the new guns have adequate accuracy, if in fact they do. Remember that your resident FTOs (field training officers) and the better marksmen in the department have a disproportionate influence on the opinions and confidence of the cops they work with vis-à-vis firearms.

The department should gain as much input as possible from other agencies that have been using the pistol in question. Within a few years of the 1967 adoption of the Model 39, Illinois State Police armorers had become more knowledgeable of the real-world performance of the S&W automatic than anyone at the factory. The manufacturer will always tell you their gun is as good as gold. You need input from unbiased sources.

Field-test the gun with duty hollowpoint ammunition. Such guns as the HK P9S and the first two generations of S&W autoloaders did not function reliably with hollowpoints, nor (at this writing) do certain standard production runs of Colt and Browning automatics. Colt's stainless Governments and Combat Elites do, however, come factory throated, as does the grey finished "NATO" version of the Browning Hi-Power, and feed hollowpoints reliably.

*Department should use all available input for testing. Left to right are Ruger armorer Rick Devoid, Lt. Ayoob, and gunsmith Nolan Santy. P-85 was ultimately approved as optional weapon for Ayoob's department.*

*Testing of potential service auto should include reliability and accuracy testing with all available duty and training ammo. Shown is a small selection of the many assorted rounds the author put through Ruger P-85 test gun.*

It is imperative that duty loads, not generic GI hardball ammo, be used in the testing process. All of the above guns that developed reputations for jamming with hollowpoints had enviable reliability records with round-nose, full metal jacket ammo that would cause ricochet and overpenetration hazards, and stopping failures, in street police shootings.

This writer has been a firearms instructor since 1972, lately teaching up to 1,500 personnel per year, most of whom were police instructors who would go on to train many other officers, and who at the time of training had a wealth of their own information and experience to share. One recent class was typical: 24 students were responsible for training more than 6,900 other personnel in police firearms and officer survival annually. While teaching 20 people for a week I will see about 10,000 rounds fired from all manner of police handguns. From that collective experience came the following recommendations in selection of the semiautomatic pistol for police service and personal self defense:

*Most Reliable Semiautomatic Pistol: Heckler and Koch P7 Series.* My own test sample went over 4,000 recorded rounds of jacketed ammo, mostly hollowpoint, without a single failure to cycle and fire, *and without being cleaned or field-stripped.* The author knows of no other handgun, revolver or auto, that can approach that level of reliable functioning under extreme abuse and neglect.

In my experience, the P7 also fits the small hand extremely well (8-shot model) and has very low recoil due to its gas operation and low bore axis. It is extremely compact and ideal for concealed carry. Adopted by New Jersey State Police (P7M8) after it beat all the competition, it has since proven itself trustworthy in the hands of thousands of troopers whose union president, Tom Iskzyricki, tells me the rank and file are enthusiastically confident with it. Power performance of the issue Remington 115-grain JHP 9mm. load has been satisfactory. The squeeze-cocking mechanism forces the shooter to take a firm hold, and I have found the P7 to be an "orthopedic pistol" that makes the poor shooter shoot well and the good shooter perform superlatively. While there were

*Author considers these among the first choices in police autoloaders. Top to bottom, the SIG-Sauer P-226 is perhaps easiest "transition gun" when going from the service revolver; Beretta 92F is perhaps the best made in terms of workmanship; the Glock-17 is the easiest to learn to shoot well; Smith & Wessons like this 459 are perhaps the safest of all police autos; and HK's P7 in his experience is the most reliable in the face of neglect and abuse.*

a few accidental leg-shootings which occurred when officers tried to holster the gun with the cocker still squeezed and their fingers on the trigger (the finger stopped at the edge of the holster, and the gun and trigger kept moving downward) this syndrome was eliminated with increased training. H&K believes that the squeeze cocker is a weapon retention advantage in that someone unaccustomed to the gun who got it away from an officer could not make it fire. This writer does not anticipate anyone pulling his gun from him and then holding it like a wimp, and would expect it to go off in the attacker's death grip. However, at least one and arguably two New Jersey troopers were saved from death when suspects disarmed them and pointed the P7M8s at them but could not make them fire.

The P7M13, with a 14-round capacity, is as reliable as the P7M8 in this writer's experience and that of the Utah State Patrol, which issues it. However, the combination of the fat, staggered magazine and the squeeze cocker make it a large-girthed pistol not ideally suited for small hands.

*Safest All Around Semiautomatic Pistol: Smith & Wesson Third Generation.* The double-action first shot of the S&W auto reduces the likelihood of an accidental discharge under stress. The option of locking the thumb catch on "safe" has saved innumerable lives when suspects got S&W autos away from cops but couldn't figure out how to make them go off. Unique among double-action police automatics at this time, the S&W also has a magazine disconnector safety which renders the chambered round incapable of being fired if the magazine is released. Several officers in Illinois State Police, Las Vegas Metro PD, Salt Lake City, and elsewhere are alive because of that feature: if the gun is being pried from the officer's hand as he is overpowered, the magazine release becomes a "deactivating button" that "kills" the gun's ability to fire if someone does get it from him.

The breakdowns, chronic jamming problems, and accidental discharges when dropped that plagued the first generation (model 39) and second generation (model 59 and 39-2) pistols have all been remedied in the current "3D" models available from S&W: the .45 caliber 645 and the 9mm. 439, 639, 459, 659, 469, and 669. All can be carried concealed in well-chosen holsters, and the 439, 639, 469, and 669 in particular are designed for compactness.

Shortcomings? All have light magazine release springs (4 lb. instead of the industry standard 8 lb.), but this is easily remedied. None of the S&W autos are famous for their accuracy and the 439, 459, 639, and 659 in particular are known for their mediocre grouping ability.

*Author feels the S&W model 645 is the pistol that will "make" the .45 auto as a domestic service weapon. Stainless steel construction, extreme feed reliability with hollowpoints, and desirable double action first shot with additional safety features combine with excellent stopping power and low penetration to create an ideal police/defense package.*

*Easiest Autoloader to Shoot: The Glock 17.* Light and handy due to its plastic-intensive construction, a natural pointer due to its sharply angled grip, and easy to control due to its unique "safe action" single action trigger, the Glock requires no safety catches or decocking levers to be operated. Point gun, pull trigger. It is as simple to fire as a revolver, actually simpler since the trigger stroke is shorter and more controllable.

This pistol has been adopted by the City of Miami police and adopted or authorized by numerous other organizations. It is extremely reliable with hollowpoints and has been known to go 2,000-3,000 rounds without a malfunction, without being cleaned. It is compact and easy to carry and fits small hands well.

Disadvantages? There is no "proprietary nature to the user" feature, and with some holsters, is prone to accidental discharge if thrust into the scabbard with the finger still on the trigger. For police use, it should be ordered **only** with the optional 8 lb. to 10 lb. trigger pull.

*Easiest Autoloader to Switch to from Revolvers: The SIG-Sauer System.* Designed by SIG of Switzerland and produced by Sauer of West Germany, this system has no external safety catch. It has a double-action first shot for greater safety when taking suspects at gunpoint. It is extremely accurate.

In order, the most popular SIG-Sauers among uniformed cops are the P-226 16-shot 9mm., the P-220 8-shot .45, and the P-225 9-shot 9mm. The similar, smaller P-230 in .380 is popular for off-duty wear.

The author's experience is that all SIG-Sauer guns are extremely reliable, and at this writing all current production guns are factory throated for hollowpoints, which was not the case in the first years they were marketed. The P-220 is in service with numerous municipal departments such as Huntington Beach, CA, the Department of Energy, and the Arizona highway patrol (where troopers can choose this gun or the P-226 9mm.).

The P-226 is in service with RCMP SWAT, the Secret Service protective detail and other Federal agencies, is a very popular optional gun with U.S. Marshal's Service, and has performed splendidly with such street patrol organizations as Elizabeth, New Jersey.

Its strength is its weakness, in this writer's opinion: many experts feel that the absence of a safety catch prevents failure to release the lever and guarantees a fast, reflexive first shot by the officer. However, that same absence of a safety catch obviates the "proprietary nature to the user" feature that the collective police experience has found to be such an important advantage of the conventional autoloader.

The author has seen a few frame failures in the SIG service pistols, all of which are readily made good on by the manufacturer. All the SIGs are extremely rugged and reliable pistols.

*Most Field Proven Police Autoloader: Colt .45 Automatic.* Since 1911 in the hands of military police, Texas Rangers, and numerous domestic police departments, the "army automatic" has proven itself a reliable performer. Properly carried cocked and locked, which gives it an unbeaten speed to an accurate first shot under stress and a higher rate of hit potential in the terror of a gunfight than any revolver or double-action auto, its "always cocked" nature also somewhat increases the risk of an accidental discharge under emotional pressure. For this reason, its use is best limited to seasoned veterans and experts.

Purchased new, best performance is found in the Combat Elite and Stainless Government models, which are factory throated. Some other models do not feed hollowpoints as well. The Officer's Model has not, in the many samples that have gone through this writer's classes, lived up to the reliability standard the bigger Colts have established.

In the hands of such highly trained units as LAPD SWAT, the Colt .45 auto has proven itself to be the "ultimate gunfighting pistol" it has

*Colt .45 automatic, like this one fine-tuned for police duty by Bill Wilson, gets author's vote as most street proven police/self-defense autoloader.*

been called by such private authorities as Jeff Cooper and Ray Chapman. However, being designed for killing enemy soldiers rapidly instead of for taking criminal suspects at gunpoint, it is not the best choice for general issue to all field personnel. This writer believes it to be an excellent sidearm for the officer who has proven himself cool under stress and can qualify at Master level of gun handling on demand.

*Best Made Police Autoloader: Beretta 92F.* Colts and Smiths sometimes come out rough. SIGs have a lot of stampings. For pure workmanship, one cannot beat the hand-forged parts of the big Beretta pistol, whose slide action also tends to be the smoothest of any, out of the box. Early samples showed high malfunction and failure rates, but in the past few years Beretta has decisively cured that problem. Since the discontinuation of the superbly accurate HK P9S, the Beretta is probably tied with the HK P7 as the most accurate out of the box police service 9mm. auto, with the SIG a very close second. Current samples feed hollowpoints without fail.

Even the compact version is a big gun with a long trigger reach, not ideally suited for general issue to officers with small hands. Still, cops who try Berettas vote with their wallets. When LAPD officers were given their choice of Beretta or Smith and a chance to try both at the range, the great majority bought Berettas. Testing by field officers on Las Vegas Metro showed an overwhelming preference for the Beretta; the S&W was retained only when the manufacturer provided all new model 659 pistols in even trade for worn old model 59s. The strongest point in favor of the Smith in the patrolman reviews this writer was shown at LVMPD was that the S&W had a magazine disconnector safety and also that the Beretta, unlike the Smith, had a red dot to show when the safety was off. It was felt by a minority that both those factors could compromise the "proprietary nature to the user" feature that LVMPD cops well knew had kept their brother officers alive when their model 59s had been taken from them.

The Beretta has also been known to trip its takedown latch when inserted into certain types of shoulder holster, according to reports, rendering the gun inoperable. Nonetheless, this excellent weapon—the first 9mm. chosen to replace the 1911 Colt .45 auto in the U.S. military service—is the most beautifully manufactured police autoloader at this writing. Its smoothness and reliability inspire confidence in the men of the Connecticut State Police, the Wyoming State Police, and many other officers who are issued it as the only approved sidearm.

*Most Cost Effective Police Autoloader: Ruger P-85.* In prototype, this 9mm. pistol was perhaps the only 9mm. auto with worse accuracy than the model 39 Smith & Wesson; this writer sent his sample to BarSto for a new barrel to improve grouping. Bill Ruger delayed production, however, until he had developed a method of tightening the slide to improve accuracy without compromising reliability.

Today's P-85 will equal the accuracy of a Smith & Wesson with 100% feeding reliability in this writer's opinion, firing even weak handloads that were virtually designed to jam a 9mm. pistol. The controls could have better human engineering—a smaller slide release and a larger safety catch—but the gun is fit for fighting duty as it comes from the box. This 16-shot 9mm. (actually, 17-shot in this writer's experience) has a double-action first shot . . . and dramatically undersells the rest of the field.

A Ruger P-85 costs less than half the price of a SIG P-226 or Beretta 92, less than a third the price of an HK P7, and distinctly undersells even the S&W series at this writing. Money saved on the gun, if spent instead on practice ammo and combat shooting/officer survival tactics training, makes a great deal of sense. A thoroughly trained officer entering a danger scene with a Ruger P-85 is far more likely to survive than a marginally trained cop going into the same dark place with a $2,500 combat custom automatic.

*Department should not be the first to adopt a new gun. Here, in the early '80s, author test fires a toolroom prototype of S&W 645 during Ordnance Expo at the LA Police range. This early gun jammed frequently. Production 645s, however, have been extremely reliable and are excellent service pistols. Photo courtesy Los Angeles Police Revolver and Athletic Club.*

*In multi-season areas, usability in extreme cold or other local weather conditions should be tested prior to approval. Here Lt. Ayoob begins a qualification course with Bren Ten service auto in 10mm. at below zero temperature.*

# SEMIAUTOMATIC PISTOLS FOR FEMALE PERSONNEL

Affirmative Action Hiring had a profound impact on law enforcement weapons training when it brought petite females with proportionate-size hands, and small statured male officers, into a profession that was once the preserve of large, powerfully built men. In 1980, this writer was the sole expert witness on firearms training for the plaintiffs in *Christine Hansen, et. al., v. Federal Bureau of Investigation.* Hansen had led a class action suit of several female agents who had been fired for failure to qualify on the revolver course at the FBI Training Academy in Quantico. Largely as a result of that testimony, the court ordered FBI to rehire the fired agents at full back pay, and "revise and update the obsolete and sexist firearms training" of the Bureau. This process began the following year, with the so-called "New Methods of FBI Training."

When the small hand encloses the large revolver, certain problems occur. The classic US police revolver is the K-frame Smith & Wesson (model 10, 19, etc.) that was introduced in 1899 as the "Smith & Wesson Military & Police .38 Special." As I argued in *Hansen*, descendants of that weapon (the gun in question in *Hansen* was the S&W model 10-6 .38) harkened to a day when the police officer was an average or larger than average size male, and the gun was designed to fit such hands. The petite female will have a hand approximately one finger digit shorter in length than that of the average male.

The double action revolver is designed so that, with the barrel in line with the forearm and the upper recurve of the grip in the center of the web of the hand, the farthest joint of the index finger can rest on the center of the trigger. This gives the trigger finger maximum leverage for a smooth stroke. With the average size male hand, it also positions the rest of the hand to hold the 12½ to 44 ounce revolver steady while 192 ounces of trigger pressure are applied against it. (The lightest police revolver, S&W's Airweight Chief Special, weighs 12½ ounces; the heaviest in conventional use, the 4″ Colt Python .357, weighs 44 ounces, and the average trigger pull on a double action revolver is twelve pounds.)

If a small hand grasps oversize double-action revolvers, one of two things will happen: either the trigger finger can't reach forward enough for leverage, and the small-handed officer can't pull the trigger, OR, the hand has to be compromised into an "H-grip". This is the position in which the hand is curled around the side of the gun so the finger can be appropriately positioned on the trigger, but the rest of the gun is not properly positioned vis-à-vis the hand and arm. The H-grip worked all right with recoilless .22 target pistols, but with a service weapon, the barrel is now in line with the base joint of the thumb instead of the forearm, and the hand does not have a controlling purchase on the grip of the recoiling handgun. The grip must be readjusted between shots, precluding effective accurate rapid fire shooting. It also causes recoil to be directed into the joint of the thumb, creating "artificial arthritis".

Ironically, the GI Colt .45 automatic in the Government Model, Officer's Model, Commander series and military 1911A1 configuration **are much better adapted to the female hand.** This is because all these guns have the shorter trigger with cutaway frame behind the trigger guard that was designed for the "A1" modification of the 1911 service pistol in 1928, to accommodate soldiers with smaller hands. We have found that the petite female hand, one digit shorter in the fingers than an adult male's of average height, adapts perfectly to these guns. Gun enthusiasts in the audience are reminded that the average or larger male usually needs to fit a "long trigger" to the conventional Colt automatic to make it fit his hand. Given the fact that the short, light trigger of these pistols can be manipulated with the first pad instead of the first joint of the index finger, we have even more room to work with.

In 1988, John Bowman of the Illinois Police Training Institute recorded the case of a petite female officer who could fire no better than 316 out of a 500 point course with her duty S&W .38 K-frame revolver fitted with the smallest available grips. Bowman switched her to a Colt Government Model .45 service automatic and her score shot up to a credible 434.

The Colt .45 automatic has allowed numerous women to win combat pistol matches against males. I have trained petite females who simply could not grasp a double action service revolver effectively, to shoot high scores with a Colt .45 automatic. Properly grasped, the pistol is not nearly as difficult to control as is commonly believed. The Colt .45 has only 17 pounds of free recoil, and even a petite female who is healthy will register at least 50-60 pounds of strength on a hand dynamometer. When she is in a stable firing position with her shoulders forward of her pelvis, her under-100 lb. body weight is more than enough to overpower the recoil of a .45 automatic.

My daughter Cathy, age ten at this writing, has no trouble firing the short-triggered, factory stock Colt Series '80 Government Model .45 auto that I carry on police duty. She is 4'9" tall and weighs approx-

*Autoloaders generally perform better than revolvers in the hands of competent females. Janet Hartman of Ohio Peace Officer Training Academy is one of the nation's leading woman instructors. Her 9mm. S&W model 659 is caught by author's camera at the instant of discharge; note flame at muzzle, slide beginning to unlock and travel rearward to cycle.*

imately 75 pounds. I have trained adult females as petite as 4'8" and 85 lb. to handle such pistols well enough to outshoot most males in their classes.

Even more suitable for many petite females is the Heckler and Koch P7 or P7M8 9-shot 9mm. pistol. The 13 shot version (M13) is too thick in the grip for many large males to grasp firmly, let alone those with small hands. However, the conventional P7 combines a low bore axis and an ingenious gas system to reduce recoil to .380 pocket pistol level, with a trigger that is easy to reach, and a squeeze cocking mechanism that forces them to hold the weapon firmly. I use the P7 at the LFI ranges as an "orthopedic remedial pistol" for small-handed males AND females who don't shoot well with double action revolvers, and almost invariably, they will rise from a failing score with the service revolver to top fourth in the class with a P7.

I have little patience with the police chief who says, "We issue the heavy frame revolver, period, and if someone can't qualify with it, they're out." Such a chief has become mired in protocol and forgotten what his job is about. His job is (a) to guarantee the public safety, and (b) to do so via his inspired command of X number of field officers who can do the job to the best of their abilities. To force all officers to carry a gun designed for a large male hand is like forcing all of them to drive a patrol car with the seats adjusted for a 6'4" male: he will make many otherwise competent officers incapable of handling their equipment and performing their job.

If that chief has the sexist goal of allowing only large males on his department, mandating a large-frame revolver will succeed almost as well as mandating that fixed seat position for large males in all the patrol cars. He'll have all large males . . . but he *won't* be getting the maximum efficiency from the personnel available to him.

Thus, the properly selected auto pistol permits maximum performance — sometimes, high performance hitherto thought to be impossible — from the petite female or small statured male officer. However, certain popular police autoloaders won't necessarily achieve that. Most double action police pistols have very long "trigger reach," and remember, medium-size *revolvers* of double action design have enough trigger reach to make them untenable for the small hand. This writer has average male hands, and finds the reach on the HK P9S far too long in double action carry. I carry all four of my P9S pistols in their optional cocked and locked (single action) position, and set two of my three national records with a P9S in that mode. Edith Almeida set the record of consecutive High Female awards at the Bianchi Cup International Pistol Championships with a P9S carried cocked and locked. The tall and graceful Almeida's height, weight, and hand-size correspond to the average adult US male's.

The petite female with limited upper arm and hand strength may, however, have trouble operating the slide of a semiautomatic. We have found the following answers to that problem.

No. 1: Much of the resistance encountered when trying to pull the slide to the rear is caused by the mainspring or hammer spring when the hammer is in the down position. If the hammer is cocked prior to drawing back the slide, much or most of this resistance is eliminated.

No. 2: If design of the pistol does not permit cocking the hammer, the student can usually operate the gun with the technique developed by pistol champion Mike Plaxco, in which the left hand grasps the top of the slide by the operating grooves, and the inside of the left hand is pressed against the chest beneath the left breast . . . the right hand and shoulder now push forward against the resisting left hand, forcing the slide back.

As an instructor, this writer has often had to deal with the loss of confidence experienced by the female recruit or officer. Having to perform physical training and marksmanship tasks built around male equipment and male strengths, she often feels that she has three strikes against her. Some of the male students (particularly those she has outperformed in the academic phases of the police academy) often take this opportunity to make fun of her. I have found no "quick fix" that better sets things in perspective than to hand that female my Colt .45 automatic and have her rip eight heavy bullets downrange into the center of the target. As she is thinking to herself, "Wow! I CAN hit that damn thing," she'll hear me telling the male students, "This baby fox just shot better than you studs with a gun twice as powerful as your .38 revolvers! Stop making fun of her and let's see if any of *you* are man enough to shoot a group like she just shot!" This tends to get the male students' minds back on their own performance, to shut off sexist remarks, and to build new confidence in the female student.

Disabled persons also have need of weapons that will be recommended by police supervisors. These include injured or wounded police officers assigned to limited duty during their recovery period, retired officers of senior citizen status, and the many law-abiding private citizens whose gun permits are signed by police chiefs and who ask police officers for recommendations on what guns to use.

The trend-setting editor (now editor-emeritus) of the nation's first and most famous police professional journal, *Law and Order,* is Frank MacAloon. Few people knew that Frank was paralyzed from the neck down due to a swimming accident in his teens. He had just enough use of his hands to shave and handle a cup of coffee. He didn't have the strength to pull a revolver's trigger double action, or to work the slide on an auto pistol. When he asked me for references on a suitable defense weapon during the time I wrote for him, I suggested the tip-up Beretta model 950 series automatic. This was an auto pistol of .25 or .22 Short caliber with a single action trigger; he could easily flip off the safety and fire, even with debilitated hands. Also, the slide didn't have to be actuated to chamber a round. Instead, the light touch of the thumb on the tip-up button would flip the rear of the barrel upward to allow a cartridge to be inserted by hand. When Beretta updated that design to their .380 automatic, I recommended he upgrade to it.

My daughter at the age of eight began pistol shooting with Beretta 950 .22 Short and .25 automatics, using that tip-up feature. Not only was it easy for her weak, small hands to operate, but the safety factor was far greater than the conventional automatic, which is operated by drawing the slide back and forth and which allows a cartridge to "hide" in the chamber beneath the shadow of the overhanging slide. I recommend this Beretta design most strongly for senior citizens, cops off on work-related disability, and other "Good Guys" who have need to be armed and do not have the strength to operate a conventional revolver or autoloader.

The bottom line is this: for the petite female or other person who for reasons involving physical size or strength is not able to prove competence with a conventional police style revolver, a properly selected semiautomatic pistol can make all the difference. As I told the Court in *Hansen*, the question is not whether this person can operate a standard issue service revolver. The question is whether this person, who has already passed the other tests of criminal record, character background check, psychological profile, and preparedness to deal with violence, can be outfitted with a safe, police-proven weapon that will allow them to engage multiple armed opponents with accurate rapid fire and neutralize them before they can harm innocents. If this can't be done with a revolver and CAN be done with a good service automatic, then logic demands the automatic be allowed for them.

Indeed, if one were to take the worst-shooting petite female in the recruit class, equip her with an appropriate automatic, and give her a day with a master police handgun instructor who had an open mind, one suspects that her original instructor would not want to bet his money *or* his career on the outcome of a challenge match a day later, with her using her new automatic in a fast-shooting scenario against him using his large framed revolver.

I for one stand ready to take such bets . . . I haven't lost money on them yet.

# AUTOLOADER QUALIFICATION COURSES

The department that permits autoloading handguns has certain concerns that might not be present if only revolvers were authorized. These include ability to safely unload and load a handgun of more complex design; the responsibility to ascertain that magazines work at all stages of charging from fully loaded to nearly empty; to make certain that magazines are not abused during the reloading process; to familiarize the officers with jam-clearing; and to make certain that the officers have been indoctrinated in barricade firing techniques that will not cause the pistol to jam from friction.

*After in-service qualification, tactical scenarios are beneficial. Since some auto pistols have easier triggers than revolvers, emphasis should be in keeping the gun in safe direction as officer moves. Here lead officer Janet Hartman comes up to fire from low ready position while Lt. Ayoob, in backup role, holds Colt .45 auto in high ready to keep muzzle from crossing his partner.*

*Auto pistol training should reinforce advantages of new gun. In this rapid fire relay, .45 autos are still blazing while revolver shooter (3rd from camera) has run out of ammo.*

**Safe loading/unloading.** The charging and un-charging of a revolver is simplicity itself, but with the autoloader, cartridges can "hide" in firing chambers and magazines can fail to eject. Cartridges can also fail to chamber and magazines can fail to fully seat during the loading process.

Thus, the author suggests a "lukewarm range" as opposed to a "hot range" or "cold range" for in-service qualification of veteran officers armed with autoloaders. The three range concepts are best defined as follows:

COLD RANGE: Guns are completely unloaded when the officer comes to the line, and will be loaded only upon the range officer's command. Officer will usually finish the designated exercise by shooting the weapon empty, offering the empty gun for range officer inspection before he holsters it without reloading again.

HOT RANGE: Guns are loaded when the officer arrives and will remain constantly loaded throughout the training. The officer will reload before holstering after every designated firing exercise, and will leave the range loaded.

LUKEWARM RANGE: The officer will begin with the weapon **unloaded**, and will load only on range officer's command, when on the line. However, after every designated exercise, the officer will finish by fully reloading and covering the target. Then, on the range officer's command, **he will unload the live weapon**, present it for range officer inspection, and holster the empty gun. At the conclusion of the day's training, the weapons will be cleaned under supervision and reloaded with fresh duty ammo before the officer leaves the training center.

The rationale for this is simple. We found that the cold range was the most court-defensible in the event of a training accident, and also by far the safest for training of beginners (newcomers to the gun itself, or revolver shooters using autos for the first time). However, it did not condition the officer to automatically reload at the conclusion of a shooting situation. Since the gun was always fired empty the cold range also failed to drill the officer in safe unloading of a live weapon.

The hot range in theory reduces horseplay since "all guns are treated as if they're loaded because they ARE loaded." Personally, the writer has not found this to be true. Also, many hot ranges have exercises that force the officer to run completely out of ammo, thus violating the rule of always reloading fully before he finishes on the line. Acutely aware of his empty gun, such an officer tends to go behind the firing line and reload at the first opportunity, often in an unsafe manner. Also, like the cold range, the hot range fails to indoctrinate the officer in safe unloading of a fully charged weapon. Finally, it would be most difficult to convince a jury of laymen that requiring all guns to always be loaded was anything but unsafe, since it violates their precepts of gun safety developed in the military, Hunter Safety training, etc.

LFI developed the lukewarm range concept in an effort to combine the advantages of both hot and cold ranges with the disadvantages of neither, with one important bonus.

Lukewarm range safety is every bit as pristine as the cold range . . . instant reloading and covering of the danger zone is taught just as effectively as on the hot range . . . plus, UNLIKE THE OTHER TWO, THE LUKEWARM RANGE TRAINS THE OFFICER UNDER SUPERVISION TO SAFELY UNLOAD A LIVE SERVICE PISTOL. A high percentage of accidental discharges with semiautomatic pistols involves a mistake made in the unloading process. Therefore, the lukewarm range is the best preventative for that type of accident, and also the ultimate court-proofing of a department sued in the wake of such an incident.

**Magazine function must be tested at all stages of loading, from one round to full capacity.** We in the trade find that some auto pistol magazines have enough spring tension to work well when loaded to full capacity, but if the magazine spring has "taken a set" due to poor metallurgy or overlong compression, it may run out of power and start causing jams when the officer has shot his load down to only one or two rounds in the magazine. Thus, at various points in the training and qualification, the duty magazines should ALL be fired completely empty. This also confirms that each magazine will lock the slide open when empty.

At the same time, certain pistols will feed well with only six rounds in the gun, but the springs may be TOO compressed when the gun is fully loaded for the first round to cycle out of the magazine after the chambered round has been fired. We have seen Devel 8-shot Colt .45 magazines that would not feed the topmost round when fully loaded. We have seen S&W model 39 magazines that, when loaded with 8 shots plus the ninth chambered round as per factory specs not only might cause feeding problems with the first shot out of the magazine, but could be difficult to even insert into the pistol with the slide in battery. We have seen similar problems with the 469/669 and model 59/659/459 pistols. These problems in the S&W autos are usually solved simply by loading each magazine with one round less than the stated capacity. Almost from the beginning, Illinois State Police found that their model 39s and later their model 439s worked much more reliably with only seven rounds in each magazine, and for years their troopers have been ordered to carry them that way. Likewise, we have encountered several "14-shot" Browning Hi-Power 9mm.s that would frequently malfunction when fully loaded, but worked perfectly when only twelve rounds were in the magazine and a thirteenth in the firing chamber.

In Heckler and Koch police autos, we have yet to see a P7, P7M8 or P7M13 that did not work perfectly with the stated capacity of 8 rounds in the magazine and a ninth in the chamber, (or 13 and 1 with the M13) and the P9S .45 seems to work well at its 7+1 factory-stated capacity. However, about half the P9S 9mm. magazines we've encountered will cause problems if fully loaded to 9 rounds plus the tenth in the chamber, while the problem is usually relieved if the same magazine is loaded with eight and a ninth round is in the chamber. The Colt .45 series of police autoloaders seems to work fine when fully loaded with the stated "seven in the magazine, eighth round in the chamber" ammo complement. This is compromised only with some of the aftermarket "national match magazine followers," which occasionally reduce the reliable magazine capacity to six rounds.

Thus, for obvious reasons, at least half the course of qualifying fire should be done at full capacity to test the capability of the magazines at full spring compression, and half of it should be done "running the gun dry" to test the reliability of the magazine springs at minimum tension. This is best done with a mix of tactical reloading and speed reloading, since the dumping of a partially-loaded magazine on hard ground during a speed reload can damage the magazine. Empty magazines can be dropped without worry of their being bent or damaged, since they are now light enough to land with little impact. They will be compromised by this type of training only if someone steps on them or if they are filled with sand, mud, or snow.

This danger to the magazines led the prestigious Smith & Wesson Academy at one time to recommend that all qualification be done with specially-allocated, expendable "range magazines", and that the officer's duty magazines never be used for qualification, to keep them out of harm's way. This writer **profoundly disagrees:** only routine and repeated qualification will make certain that the officer's duty magazines are in fact working properly. THE OFFICER SHOULD QUALIFY WITH THE DUTY EQUIPMENT, AND THE RANGEMASTER AND RANGE OFFICERS SHOULD INSPECT GUN AND MAGAZINES AFTER MANDATORY CLEANING OF BOTH BEFORE THE OF-FICER RETURNS FROM THE RANGE TO THE STREET WITH HIS WEAPON LOADED WITH FRESH DUTY AMMUNITION.

All officers should be routinely re-familiarized with jam clearing. In each qualification, rangemasters should force the officer to go through an exercise solving double-feed, stovepipe, dead round, failure to go to battery, partially-inserted magazine, bullet stuck in barrel, and ejec-tion failure problems. These reactions must become second nature if the officer is to have confidence carrying the semiautomatic.

Frankly, this writer thinks all revolver-armed officers should at least once a year pass a drill in which they solve the problems of frozen cylinder, extruded primer, bullet caught between barrel and cylinder, rounds not fully seated in the chambers, and spent casings caught under the cylinder's ejection star. It is generally true that while the autoloader is somewhat more likely to malfunction, its failures can usually be cleared by hand, while revolver malfunctions usually require the ministrations of either a very highly trained weapons expert, or an armorer.

**Barricade firing techniques.** Because the slide can easily come into contact with a vertical wall, the officer should be drilled in techniques that keep the recoiling slide clear of that impeding and friction-producing surface. The slight angle of the Cirillo Hold is an excellent choice for the auto-equipped officer, whether he is shooting from the strong side OR the weak side.

With all autos except the left-ejecting Walther P-5, the gun throws its spent casings to the right. This means that the right- OR left-handed

officer firing from a left-side barricade stands an excellent chance of
a shell coming out of the ejection port, hitting the wall, and bouncing
back into the pistol, jamming it.

*Considerable in-service training should emphasize use of cover. Ayoob supervises as these Venezuelan
policemen use indoor range shooting benches to simulate low cover. Duty pistols are Browning
Hi-Powers. Note breath mask author uses on indoor ranges.*

This does not usually occur on the conventional firing range, where
the barricade is a flat piece of wood or metal. In the real world, however,
the barricade is likely to be the side of a wall, and there is just no room
for the shell to fly clear. We have seen it happen on the training range,
and it could happen easily on the street as well. This is why ALL officers, southpaw or right-hand dominant, should learn the Cirillo Cant
for firing around left-side cover. We also suggest that at least part of
the barricade shooting involve an actual, long surfaced wall instead of
just a flat plank.

## COURSES OF FIRE

Several training programs have been built around the auto pistol. Useful drills include the "Advanced Military" and others from the sport of IPSC. A query to a local gun dealer can put you in contact with the nearest IPSC club, which can furnish you with a list of the latest approved matches.

The author's preferred solution is to take the existing recommended course for the revolver, and cut the time in half when it is fired with the auto. This builds the officer's confidence, showing him that he can do twice what was once expected of him. It also allows the chief to show his peers and superiors how much the officer's performance has improved since he authorized the more modern pistols. Triple time is not beyond expectation, and using a high capacity 9mm. auto without reloading, five times standard speed on the FBI's Tactical Revolver Course can be achieved by the highest-performing officers.

An officer so certified has qualified to twice or more the prevailing standard of care in police combat shooting. There is no better proof of competence to forestall unmeritorious civil action brought against the department or the individual in the wake of a shooting incident.

Such courses can be shot for basic "qualification of record," with more challenging courses involving physical movement and practical use of field cover augmenting the officer's training on a pass/fail or familiarization basis.

# SUGGESTED READING

| | |
|---|---|
| *In The Gravest Extreme* by Massad F. Ayoob | $ 9.95 |
| *StressFire* by Massad F. Ayoob | $ 9.95 |
| *The Semiautomatic Pistol in Police Service and Self-Defense* by Massad F. Ayoob | $ 9.95 |
| *Fundamentals of Modern Police Impact Weapons* by Massad F. Ayoob (Hardcover) | $15.95 |
| *Hit the White Part* by Massad F. Ayoob | $ 7.95 |
| *Gunproof Your Children / Handgun Primer* by Massad F. Ayoob | $ 4.95 |
| *Police Handgun Manual* by Bill Clede (Hardcover) | $13.95 |
| *Police Shotgun Manual* by Bill Clede (Hardcover) | $13.95 |
| *Police Nonlethal Force Manual* by Bill Clede (Hardcover) | $15.95 |
| *The Combat .45 Automatic* by Bill Wilson | $12.95 |
| *Mastertips* by Jon Winokur | $11.95 |
| *Shoot To Win* by John Shaw | $11.95 |
| *You Can't Miss* by John Shaw and Michael Bane | $11.95 |
| *The Pride Method* by John Pride and Jon Winokur | $ 4.95 |
| *Executive Safety and International Terrorism: A Guide for Travellers* by Anthony J. Scotti (Hardcover) | $21.95 |
| *The Tactical Edge* by Chuck Remsberg (Hardcover) | $35.95 |
| *Street Survival* by Chuck Remsberg, Ron Adams, and Tom McTernan (Hardcover) | $25.95 |
| *Life Without Fear* by Mike Dalton and Mickey Fowler | $11.95 |
| *Bluesteel & Gunleather* by John Bianchi | $12.00 |
| *Mothers and Others Be Aware* by Donna Miller | $12.95 |
| *The Street Smart Gun Book* by John Farnam | $11.95 |
| *Handgun Retention System* by James W. Lindell | $17.50 |
| *Realistic Defensive Tactics* by John Peters and Takayuki Kubota | $ 9.95 |
| *Defensive Tactics with Flashlights* by John Peters | $10.00 |
| *Soft Body Armor: The Professional's Guide for Selection and Use* by Richard C. Davis and Massad F. Ayoob | $ 9.95 |
| *Official Kubotan Techniques* by Takayuki Kubota and John Peters | $ 6.95 |
| *The Persuader Baton* by Eric Chambers | $ 4.95 |
| *The Truth About Self Protection* by Massad F. Ayoob | $ 6.95 |

*Prices and availability subject to change without notice.*

Please add $2.95 to cover shipping and handling.
To order, send check or money order to **Police Bookshelf, P.O. Box 122, Concord, N.H. 03302-0122** or use your MasterCard or Visa number and call toll free 1-800-624-9049. In New Hampshire call 603-224-6814.